D0221095

The Politics of Mental Health

Banton, R.

C H

The Politics of Mental Health

Critical Texts in Social Work and the
Welfare State

General Editor: Peter Leonard

The Politics of Mental Health

Ragnhild Banton
Paul Clifford
Stephen Frosh
Julian Lousada
Joanna Rosenthall

MACMILLAN

First published 1985

Published by
Higher and Further Education Division
MACMILLAN PUBLISHERS LTD
Houndmills, Basingstoke, Hampshire RG21 2XS
and London
Companies and representatives
throughout the world

**Printed in Great Britain
at the University Press, Oxford**

British Library Cataloguing in Publication Data
The Politics of mental health.—(Critical texts
in social work and the welfare state)
1. Mental illness—Treatment
I. Title II. Banton, Ragnhild III. Series
616.89'06   RC349.8
ISBN 0–333–36128–8
ISBN 0–333–36129–6 Pbk

Contents

About the Authors

This book has been written collectively. We began as a radical mental health group in the autumn of 1979, offering talks, courses and workshops to people living and working in the London boroughs of Lambeth and Southwark. In 1981 we formed a sub-group to concentrate on writing a pamphlet on mental health issues. As our ideas became more concrete and complex, this pamphlet changed into a book, although we retained the ideal of creating something together. Every part of the book was written collectively. The ideas were generated through discussion in the group, then one or two people wrote each section, which was then discussed and re-written, often by someone else. This process was a difficult one, with divisions appearing particularly between those members of the group who were reasonably confident about writing and those who found it intimidating and worrying. We tried hard to overcome these difficulties by discussion and argument and by making our regular group meetings a forum for support as well as for criticism.

All of us are professional mental health workers. Ragnhild works with ex-psychiatric patients in a Community Day Centre; Paul is a psychologist working with adults in the health service; Stephen is a psychologist working with children and families in the health service; Julian is a social work tutor offering counselling and consultancy services to community mental health groups; Jo is a social worker running groups and providing counselling within the Family Welfare Association. All of us are currently, or have been recently, in personal psychoanalysis or psychoanalytic psychotherapy, an experience that has had a substantial impact on the ideas expressed in the book. Our political commitments range from membership of socialist parties to socialist feminist groups, but converge in our attempts to find ways to radicalise our professional practice. In doing this we have found important support from each other as we have wrestled with the concepts and implications of the book.

Acknowledgements

Many people have helped us with this book, either directly or indirectly, through inspiring us to think and work in particular ways. We would especially like to thank the other members of the Lambeth and Southwark Community Mental Health Group. We are also indebted to Paul Hoggart and Sue Holland, members of the Battersea Action and Counselling Centre, which was the predecessor of the Lambeth and Southwark group. Peter Leonard's comments after our first draft were very significant in enabling us to pull our ideas together more cogently and in forcing us to do some political work which had been carefully avoided. Steven Kennedy's editorial comments have also been helpful at various points along the way.

Finally, we would like to thank Julian and Jo's housemates for putting up with our weekly meetings for so long, and Julian's mum for lending us her house for a weekend that turned out to be important in the life of the group.

Ragnhild Banton
Paul Clifford
Stephen Frosh
Julian Lousada
Joanna Rosenthall

Editor's Introduction

Central to a socialist conception of change is the notion of *praxis*: reflecting upon the world and changing it within the same process. 'If you want to know a certain thing', Mao Tsetung writes,[1] 'you must personally participate in the struggle to change reality, to change that thing.' From a Marxist perspective, at least, the separation of theory from practice is a feature of the bourgeois social order which socialists must consistently struggle against. It follows from this notion of a human activity which unifies theory and practice that to create socialism involves 'subjective changes' in people as well as changes in 'objective' social relations, in production, reproduction, consumption, etc. 'In revolutionary activity', Marx and Engels write,[2] 'the changing of oneself co-incides with the changing of circumstances.' The relationship between two kinds of changes – in people and in material relations – is not a simple matter of the one *determining* the other, but a more complex situation of interaction. It is a pity that this complexity is not better understood for it has far-reaching implications within the politics of the Left.

But to argue that people must change as part of a transformation of the entire social order is to direct our attention to precisely how people's consciousness, including our own, is constructed within historically specific social relations. It is clear, especially to those whose occupations involve responding to the inner distress produced by these social relations, that the social construction of the individual in terms of needs and desires is a matter of great complexity. The individual is not, after all, simply *influenced* by 'external' social forces, but constructs herself and is constructed within a set of social relations which define individuality itself. Moreover, it is evident that we are not conscious of the degree of penetration which the social order imposes upon us. Indeed, the orthodox Marxist position here[3] is that this lack of awareness can only give way to a full understanding when the exploitive relationships characteristic of a class society are themselves swept away.

This problem of lack of awareness of precisely how we as individuals are socially constructed is especially significant in the field of mental health and mental illness. The dominant models of treatment are based upon an understanding of the individual as essentially *prior* to the social order rather than as being historically constructed within it: 'social factors' are seen as influencing the incidence and distribution of some mental illnesses, but the absence of a theoretical (and political) appreciation of the deeply embedded structural determinants of health and illness leads to a health care practice which remains fundamentally individualistic.

The significance of mental health as an arena of Left politics has developed steadily since the 1960s' interest in the social construction and control of deviance in general. The phenomenological and interactionist emphasis of workers in the mental health field in the 1960s onwards, of which R. D. Laing is perhaps the most famous, turned out to be too limited a basis for the revolutionary reappraisal of mental illness that was expected of it. Feminist approaches to women's mental health, with their focus on domestic and wage labour, and on the structural position of women generally in the genesis of mental illness, have proved to be a more important step forward. No progressive Left approach to mental health is conceivable today that does not attempt to take account of class, gender and ethnic relations as significant structural determinants.

But it is one thing to suggest what a Left theory and practice of mental health should aim to take account of and quite another matter to articulate in detail the very complex relationship between elements in the social order and mental states of individuals. More difficult still is to develop a practice on the basis of this understanding which is itself grounded in practice. There appear to be two alternative ways forward which present themselves to us here. First, we can attempt to develop an understanding of mental health on the exclusive theoretical and political base of socialist and feminist categories (class, labour, patriarchy, alienation, etc.) and reject any primary reliance on bourgeois psychology and psychiatry either as theory or practice. This involves creating a new psychology, an effort which is still in its infancy. Second, we can use (and possibly invert) bourgeois psychology and psychiatry for progressive, socialist and feminist ends, and in its deep commitment to psychoanalysis as a theory and a practice this book *The Politics of Mental Health* is representative of the second alternative.

In its emphasis on practice, *The Politics of Mental Health* is outstanding. A group of practitioners in the mental health field have successfully struggled together to create a coherent perspective on the contradictions and possibilities of a radical practice which deserves very wide and detailed attention. It is a book which bases itself upon a psychoanalytic account of individual development, understood within a generally Marxist perspective on ideology and material relations. A dynamic concept of the unconscious is crucial, the authors argue, to an understanding of the social construction of individuality for such a concept is essentially dialectic, surpassing in its explanatory power notions about the passivity of individuals in the face of the imprinting of socialisation process. It is on the basis of this socially informed psychoanalytic account that the major parts of this book are founded – the detailed examination and critique of the authors' own practice in mental health and parallel fields. The result is a courageous and eminently worthwhile exploration of possibilities, problems and contradictions in practice undertaken at a self-critical level which compares most favourably with the radical rhetoric so frequently encountered. The authors are modest in their claims but are surely right in suggesting that their approach to mental health is essentially *subversive*.

There is no doubt that this book will raise many questions and debates amongst those on the Left who are committed to practice in the mental health field. It furthers some of the arguments entered into in *Personality and Ideology: Towards a Materialist Understanding of the Individual*, the book of mine which was published in this Critical Texts series in 1984. The two books differ in a number of ways: *Personality and Ideology* is essentially an introductory theoretical book, is more critical of psychoanalytic theory and places less emphasis on ideology and more on the actual material relations involved in labour processes. Both books are, however, similarly committed to the proposition that an understanding of, and response to, individual mental distress is an important part of the political agenda of the Left. The authors of *The Politics of Mental Health* mount, in my view, an overwhelmingly convincing case that mental health care is a significant arena of socialist, feminist and anti-racist practice – that it must not be vacated to the domination of bourgeois therapies, drug treatments and other methods of control and social legitimation.

This book calls on us to be profoundly self-critical of our own practice in a way which is deeply enriched by its psychoanalytic understandings. We have a responsibility to confront the challenge which the *The Politics of Mental Health* presents.

University of Warwick   Peter Leonard
August 1984

REFERENCES

1. Mao Tsetung, 'On Practice' in *Selected Readings from the Work of Mao Tsetung* (Peking: Foreign Languages Press, 1971) p. 71.
2. K. Marx and F. Engels, *The German Ideology*, ed. C. J. Arthur (London: Lawrence & Wishart, 1970) p. 95.
3. See L. Sève, *Man in Marxist Theory and the Psychology of Personality* (Brighton: Harvester Press, 1978).

Authors' Introduction

This book is about the experience of mental health workers and its relevance to both politically informed therapeutic work and wider political practice. It is founded on two beliefs: that being a socialist can have a meaning for workers in the field of mental health, and that the experience of those workers has something to offer a socialist politics. Neither of these claims may seem very controversial. After all, isn't the hallmark of socialism its recognition of the links between personal distress and social organisation? Isn't the principle well established that the personal is the political, the political the personal? The principle perhaps, but faced with the suffering of a client or the political reality of the 1980s, the uncomfortable fact is that neither of these beliefs seems so self-evidently true – a sign that theory and practice have become separated, to the detriment of both.

This separation can be inadvertently encouraged by a socialist tradition which, in opposing the stress of bourgeois theories on the centrality of the 'free individual' in constructing social relations, over-emphasises the dominance of 'objective' social forces over individual behaviour and experience. The phenomenology of personal existence is decreed a cipher; little is said about human needs, desires, hopes, fears, relationships, how they are produced and distorted by capitalism, and how they might be better in a socialist society. This neglect reinforces the stereotype of socialism as a demand for an inhuman, uniform society and vacates the ground for bourgeois theories. This means that at the sharp end of practice where the question of what to do cannot be avoided, no resistance is available to a simple 'breakdown' model of human functioning: something is wrong with someone, they are no longer well but ill, the job of the helper is to patch up the damage as best they can and to return the sufferer ('client' in the pretend-egalitarianism of social work liberalism) to a context where things will run smoothly once more.

Even among a potentially radical force, welfare helpers in direct contact with the harmful effects of social organisation, the practical force of the breakdown model and the institutions in which it is enshrined, produce an implicit acceptance of the social context as a necessary, basically stable backdrop to the vagaries of individual distress. Lip-service may be paid to faults or strains in the system, but the focus of intervention, both at the level of 'cases' and the planning of services, is the individual who breaks down, not the system itself. Where consideration is given to the social aspects of welfare it is mainly at a general level: endless debates over preventative versus curative philosophies of health planning, over whether the welfare state cares or controls. Socialist professionals, struggling to think about and carry out their jobs differently, find that they are offered no formulations that engage directly with the concepts, power relations and practices that organise their work. The result is frequently a divorce between the political perceptions a worker may have concerning the general functions of welfare, and the everyday encounters which s/he engages in with clients and which constitute the work. This can lead to a despair over the possibilities of radical work within the helping professions, or the adoption of a 'patch and make do' attitude which itself is a manifestation of the dominant breakdown model of care.

The argument that traditional political theory lacks an adequate account of the subjective preconditions for social and individual change, while individual-centred approaches lack politics, is not a new one. The attempt to extend respectability to the consideration of subjective experience has been a major theme of left-wing politics for the past fifteen years. There has been particular interest in a rapprochement between Marxism and psychoanalysis, evident in the enthusiastic reception of Marcuse's (1955) *Eros and Civilisation* by 1960s radicals, and more recently inspired by Lacan's re-reading of Freud. Additionally, the anti-psychiatry movement led by Laing and Cooper, and the growth movements of the

1960s have left a lasting legacy in their emphasis on analysing oppression in terms of what people are not allowed to do or feel rather than just in economic terms. Most approaches have translated their concern for a politics that takes into account the personal into a crude 'application' of concepts such as 'capitalism' or 'patriarchy' to the analysis of ideologies or institutions. Such applications, while not without validity, are often too general for mental health workers to use in practice; in fact, their message is often that work with individuals is marginal, if not quite as unforgivable as once thought.

Only the feminist movement has made genuine strides towards an integrated 'personal politics'. This is because it has both challenged the silences on women's position in socialist theory and practice and developed its own articulation of the ways in which social and personal realities intertwine (e.g. Mitchell, 1974; Llewelyn and Osborne, 1983) thus enabling the evolution of a positive theory and practice. Our aim with respect to mental health has been similar: not just to criticise current theory – being 'anti' psychiatry is not enough – but to begin to build a positive account of a political mental health practice.

An initial problem was what to include under the rubric 'politics of mental health'. Society impinges on people in numerous ways: through the provision (or not) of food, shelter, work, health care, the rule of law and government, education, ethical and cultural values, and so on. In the broadest sense all of these could be taken as affecting a person's 'mental health', and therefore an attempt to change any one of them could legitimately be seen as relevant to a politics of mental health. Our aim, however, has been to focus on social relations that are more directly implicated in mental health practice. This has meant paying scant attention to factors such as housing, unemployment and discrimination, which are clearly causes of considerable suffering. This is not because we do not regard struggles over social economic conditions as of primary political importance, but because our project is something different: to attempt to integrate our wider political perspective and our work experience.

Our examination of the relation between theory and practice produced a number of distinct but related questions. Can

therapy be political? How do we understand the dominant
ideologies and mental health practices in the context of late
capitalism? What do we mean by the concept of power in
mental health practice? How is it implicated in the relationships between state and citizen, man and woman, black
and white, working and ruling class? How are psychological
and social processes related? What should we do differently?

One of the difficulties in addressing any of these questions is
that they all refer simultaneously both to the micro level of
interactions between client and worker and the macro level of
the set of social and political structures and institutions within
which that interaction is taking place. This 'difficulty' is an
important characteristic of the politics of mental health, so it
is necessary to avoid separating the two levels artificially. At
the same time it is insufficient merely to point out their
existence: to analyse our work a view is required of the
relationship between the two. This is the aim of Chapters 1–3.
Having defined our perspective, it is then applied in Chapters
4 and 5 to examples of therapeutic work, and in Chapter 6 to
the overall organisation and position of mental health services. In brief then, Chapters 1–3 set out our theory, which is
then applied to the micro and macro levels in turn.

In Chapter 1 we argue that the relationship between the
individual and society can be approached through an account
of ideology that includes a positive account of power relations,
and does not reduce the individual to an effect of either. We
follow Althusser's view of ideology as the 'lived relation' to the
world, but argue that this relation is neither fixed nor
determinate and is itself contradictory. This idea is then
explored with reference to ideologies surrounding the
psychiatric hospital and the doctor–patient relationship.

In Chapter 2 we take a closer look at concepts of the
individual and of how the individual comes to be in a
relationship to society. We defend a psychoanalytic account of
development, stressing the importance of the concept of the
unconscious as more than a passive imprinting of ideology. In
Chapter 3 this is applied to different understandings of mental
health and 'illness', and it is argued that therapeutic and
political practice, while not identical, are nevertheless in-
separably linked. These chapters are strongly critical of

'essentialist' views of the individual, particularly humanistic and medical approaches.

Chapter 4 is the heart of the book: it contains a discussion of six pieces of therapeutic work, three overtly 'political', three less obviously so. A number of themes recur, particularly those of power and resistance to change. Chapter 5 takes up these themes in considering the question of what might constitute a radical therapeutic practice. One respect in which it would differ from conventional practice would be in its goal of making people conscious not only of unconscious motivations but also of the effects of ideology.

Whatever radical therapy might be, it inevitably goes on in the context of mental health practices and institutions, and these in turn have important relationships to the state, patriarchal and capitalist social relations. Chapter 6 discusses these with reference to the 'community strategy' which currently dominates thinking on the political left and right in the planning of future mental health services. We argue that the 'community' is not a natural given, but is at the centre of a number of ideological discourses, and therefore that community care and community action, while not without radical possibilities, can easily be assimilated to reactionary as well as progressive political trends.

This book does not therefore aim to *introduce* politics into mental health: the politics is already there. Our task is to explore it, to begin to develop an understanding that can inform mental health practice. In so doing we are primarily concerned with the 'microsocial' politics that are expressed in the encounter between client and helper. But within this detail there are also insights that reflect back on our understanding of politics in general, that affect our view of the processes of change and the relationship between people's experience and its social context. 'The politics of mental health', then, is our primary aim, but 'mental health and politics' is our broader view.

Finally, a word on the language used. There are problems in choosing appropriate terms in writing about 'mental health', for most have medical associations. The term 'mental health' itself, while attractive in its suggestion of well-being, connotes medicine and doctors, and can imply the sort of separation of individual from society that we reject. Neverthe-less, people do have internal states, and we use it in the same way as radical groups might use notions of positive physical health: to claim psychological health as a legitimate focus of political and personal concern. We avoid the negative psychiatric terminology of 'mental illness', preferring the term 'psychological distress'. This still leaves problems in making finer distinctions, but we have tried to limit our use of technical terms to contexts in which we are discussing a particular paradigm. In general, we use ordinary-language concepts, with all their heterogeneity, although we have used more psychoanalytic terminology as the book progresses, the case for its use having been made earlier.

The choice of political vocabulary has also caused prob-lems. Some concepts like 'power' are discussed in the text. 'Socialist' refers to activities aimed at transforming society in the direction of the redistribution of resources, the restructur-ing of power relations and the formation of a classless society. 'Radical' is occasionally used as a substitute for 'socialist', but refers more often to a politically (socialist) committed approach that challenges particular institutions or disciplines. Thus we are more likely to refer to 'radical social work' than 'socialist social work'. 'Progressive' is applied to reformist activities, that is approaches which may lack socialist commit-ment but which nevertheless oppose oppressive structures. Finally, 'feminist' can refer to a range of positions advocating the relief of women's oppression. In this book the feminist ideas advanced derive from socialist feminists and feminist psychoanalysts; we try to make clear when we are referring to the feminist movement as a whole, and when to these two elements.

Our aim has been to write clearly and accessibly, avoiding unnecessary use of complex theoretical concepts. Neverthe-less, this has not always been possible because our subject is a complex one: it is our experience that to write about 'the politics of mental health' necessarily involves re-examining what is meant by both 'politics' and 'mental health'.

1
Politics and Power

This and the following two chapters elaborate our view of the 'politics of mental health' and its relation to an overall political perspective. This chapter is concerned primarily with the problem of formulating a position that allows room for the existence of a politics of mental health – one that neither regards society as more or less irrelevant to individual psychology, seeing the latter as a product of human nature, nor regards the individual as a by-product of society. The aim here, then, is not to produce an account of the social individual, this being left to Chapter 2, but to develop a framework within which such an account can take its place.

In the first section, headed 'Three practices', the distinction is adopted between three fields of social practice, each of which can be seen to place individuals in a number of often contradictory relationships: economic, political and ideological practice. It is the last of these that we regard as being of paramount importance in understanding both individual behaviour and experience and the political place of mental health practice. Ideological relations, it is argued, are not simply relations between ideas, sets of true or false beliefs, but are material, and can be construed as codifications of power relations. This has two implications: first that individuals cannot be thought of as the merely passive recipients of ideological imprinting, and that there is therefore a need for a theory of the construction of the individual within ideological relations (the topic of Chapter 2). Secondly, an understanding is needed of how power relations are bound up with ideology. This is the subject of the section 'Discourses and power', which argues that it is insufficient to consider power as a purely negative force. Rather, power relations can be seen to have both positive and negative, objective and intersubjective aspects. This theoretical account is followed by 'Hospitals and doctors', which illustrates its relevance to analysis of two of the dominant images in mental health ideology: the psychiatric hospital, and the doctor or psychiatrist. In the final section, 'Power', some of the implications of this approach to power are outlined in relation to traditional psychoanalytic and political theory and practice.

THREE PRACTICES

'The individual and society', a subheading from countless psychology and sociology textbooks, is a beacon for bourgeois thought. Here the individual, there society; the problem is how the latter is organised to allow the former to flourish in this – so we are told – freest of all possible worlds. In contrast, the radical version emphasises the oppressive impact of society on the individual: 'capitalist social relations deform individuality'. As a slogan this may engender a warm glow of oppositional fervour: 'deform' must be bad, 'individuality' good. However, it still relies on the same separation of individual and society: here are social relations, there the individual, ripe for deforming. Conflict may arise between the one and the other, but not within them: the individual is indivisible, acted upon in some systematic way by capitalism. History is reduced to the struggle of individuals for expression of their real (undeformed) selves. More is needed of a political theory than this: not just a firmer grasp of social contradictions, but also a more specific account of how the social enters into the individual.

Socialist theory identifies three linked 'practices' as constitutive of society: economic practice (the transformation of nature), political practice (the struggle to transform social relationships) and ideological practice (the production of individual consciousness). Coward and Ellis explain that

These three practices do not account for the whole of human existence. They go a long way towards delineating a social process which does not have man at its centre, but

rather constructs man as he attempts to construct the
system.
                                     (Coward and Ellis, 1977, p. 64)

We shall be mostly concerned with the third, ideological
practice. The reasons for this can be approached through a
consideration of the other two.

Economic practice

The economic practice of capitalism is characterised by the
expansion of the means of production under conditions in
which surplus value is created through the exploitation of
labour, but controlled by a private class. It is in this context
that Marx develops most powerfully the concept of 'contradiction'. For example, it is in the interests of capital to treat
workers as interchangeable, to de-individualise them, so that
they can be exploited more fully, as in the breaking down of a
skilled craft into a number of unskilled tasks. The more this
happens, however, the more strongly workers realise their
corporate interests, their formation as a class able to oppose
the very forces that created it.

Elaborations of this theory make clear links with individual
psychology, for example the development of an 'individualist'
ideology arising from capitalism's need to have 'free' individuals to sell their labour. The economic process itself is
shown by Marx to have profound effects, best stated in the
theory of alienation. Colletti sums up Marx's position thus:

The alienation which is founded in capitalism has four main
aspects:

(1) man is alienated from the products of his activity,
    which belong to another (the capitalist);
(2) man is alienated from his productive activity itself (i.e.
    work), which is not an affirmation but rather a negation
    of his essential nature;
(3) man is alienated from his own essential nature, his
    humanity;
(4) man is alienated from other men, from the community.
                                        (Colletti, 1978, p. 429)

When extended into an account of 'late' capitalism, the analysis is even more apposite: whereas under capitalist expansion workers were required only for their labour-power so that the reproduction of labour would be the paramount concern of welfare, the situation in late capitalism manifests a further turn of the screw:

> What makes capitalist society 'late' is the ascendancy of technology – 'dead labour' – over living labour in the production process. Economically this heightens the possibility of stagnation under the weight of automatically produced commodities.
>
> (Kovel, 1981, p. 75)

It becomes a goal of capitalism to increase consumption of these commodities, to convince people that they 'need' to consume. To achieve this, the state intrudes further into the realms of individual subjectivity: whereas the physical survival of the worker was the sole 'welfare' requirement of early capitalism, now the worker has to experience her/his needs differently, and for this to occur the state must find a way to influence or 'administer' subjective experience. In some accounts (e.g. Kovel, 1981) the 'mental health industry' is one important way in which this goal is achieved.

There is in this account the beginnings of a political theory that reveals contradictions in the social fabric and provides a description of how these impinge on individual experience. However, the theory remains limited: while capitalism is analysed in terms of its oppressiveness and its internal contradictions, individuals are either left out of theory or are viewed as passive respondents to social pressure. An example of the problems generated by this limitation, particularly for 'Utopian' socialism, can be found in approaches such as that of Lukács (1971). Take the idea that a socialist revolution will bring about an end to history:

> There is no history in communist society because there is concrete sensuous human activity which is 'immediate' to itself, i.e. not 'mediated' by alienated social relations. History is the process of man's realization of his essence

and it proceeds through alienation. Experience is adequate to the social relations of communism because there is no longer alienation and therefore there is no 'riddle'.

(Hirst, 1979, p. 30)

This view implies the existence of some basic human nature which under socialism will be expressed in completely 'natural', spontaneous activity. Human subjects will interact with one another without the mediation of the social fabric, unalienated and whole. Intriguingly, this form of socialist theory is in the end non-social: its Utopian vision is of a world where society does not exist, or is reduced to the free intermingling of already formed human subjects. The difficulties of such an 'essentialist' approach are discussed in detail in Chapter 2. There is one major point to be made here. The view just described relies on an opposition between society and individual which restricts the power of social explanations unwarrantably: it leaves untheorised some central basic 'essence' of the individual, which is outside the realm of politics. Although Marx's own view of humanity's essence as the 'aggregate of social relations', and alienation as the detachment of the individual from the social process (Colletti, 1978, p. 430), is somewhat more subtle than that of Lukács, it still arguably backs down from the requirement to consider the social construction of individuality; and it is not clear that it can avoid the trap of assuming that the individual is a 'natural' entity, if only in Lukács's sense of essentially engaging in 'sensuous human activity which is "immediate" to itself'. In the arena of mental health, where one is confronted with the contradictions built into individual 'essences', this theoretical failure is particularly damaging.

Political practice

Political practice is 'the representation of the relation of power between classes and class fractions' (Coward and Ellis, 1977, p. 66): it is the realm of the state. An understanding of the state, its relations, objectives and contradictions is a necessary prerequisite for radical practice. Although this is not the place for a detailed exposition (see Corrigan and Leonard, 1978, chapter 9 for a fuller account that is linked to welfare practice) a few points should be made. First, the state can be understood as a reflection of how wealth is produced in a particular society: it is specific to the mode of production, and is thus always 'specific in time and place' (Cockburn, 1977, p. 42). Second, the state is quite simply an instrument of class domination, at the centre of the major dynamic of capitalist society, the struggle between the bourgeoisie and those it exploits, the working class:

> Because the State arose from the need to hold class antagonisms in check, but because it arose, at the same time, in the midst of the conflict of the classes, it is, as a rule, the most powerful economically dominant class which, through the medium of the State, becomes also the politically dominant class and thus acquires new means of holding down and exploiting the oppressed class.
>
> (Engels, 1968, p. 586)

The contradictions that inhere in the political arena take material form in the various organisations of class forces (trade unions, revolutionary socialist parties, etc.) but also reside in the state itself, for although the state serves the long-term interests of the ruling class, it also 'reflects the balance of class forces at any given historical moment' (Corrigan and Leonard, 1978, p. 95) and thus contains within it the pressures of class struggle.

The state does not just exercise direct control through the legislature and enforcement, but also indirectly through propaganda, the media, education and the promotion of structures such as the welfare services that institutionalise certain relationships and viewpoints. Those in the helping professions may seek, via professionalism and often illusory machinations, to distance themselves from the more overtly repressive functions of the state, where use of sanctions is explicitly in the interests of control (e.g. the police, armed forces). Yet an objective of state welfare is the production of a citizenship that is willing and able to take part in the production of profit and the consumption of goods. The provision of services is thus a way of protecting the state against class antagonisms, as well as being a response to those antagonisms. It is this contradiction that makes welfare work so important for the state and for radical practice. Welfare, mental health practice included, therefore has a large part to play in the reproduction of dominant social relations, and is vital to the state's exercise of ideological as well as political control.

Ideological practice

Although economic and political practice are essential to specifying the context and effects of mental health practice, and do themselves have significant effects on consciousness, it is ideological practice that is of most direct interest to the area of mental health, because it deals with the way the contradictions of the social world (economics and politics) are experienced by, and have a hand in constructing, individual consciousness.

Traditionally, ideology has been understood by socialists to refer to a distorted representation of the real world; sometimes, in 'vulgar' Marxism, it is argued that ideology belongs to the realm of ideas and is epiphenomenal to the materialist basis of history. This assumes that there exists a 'true' reality that is potentially available to the direct experience of the individual subject (it would be so under socialism). Under capitalism, however, the subject's view of this reality is systematically distorted by her/his class position; each class position gives rise to a certain form of ideology. 'To look for the social position of the subject is a legitimate means of analysis of the ideas subjects hold' (Hirst, 1979, p. 25); that is, the true basis of these ideas can be found in the individual's social position. There are several problems with this view of ideology, but two stand out here. First, it is alarmingly mechanical, reducing each individual subject to her/his class position and allowing no room for investigation of the intra- and interpersonal contradictions that are characteristic of people within any one class. Second, it is once again essentialist; it is through the experience of one's social position that one's consciousness is developed; in class society this consciousness is consequently false, whereas in socialist society it would be true. But the faculty of experience is above society:

it, alone among all aspects of consciousness, cannot be reduced. Experience, then can have no social explanation; there is an individual 'essence' after all. In utilising sociological reductionism and yet leaving the notion of 'experience' untheorised, the traditional approach to ideology reveals its own contradictions.

There have been several attempts to explore the theory of ideology in a more satisfactory manner. One that stands out is that of Gramsci (1971), whose work has been influential amongst feminists as well as 'Eurocommunists'. The philosopher Lucien Sève (1978) is also of interest, for although he downgrades the significance of ideological practice in the face of material relations he does make a direct attempt to address the issue of 'personality' from a Marxist perspective (see Leonard, 1984, for an admirably clear account of Sève's work). However, the approach which holds the most promise for mental health work, because of the sophistication of its concepts and their close links with psychoanalysis, is that of Althusser. This is the case despite the many problems with other aspects of Althusserian theory, some of which again make it open to the charge of essentialism (e.g. Hirst, 1979; Coward and Ellis, 1977). Here, we will pick out the central elements of Althusser's approach which make it the most promising attempt to explain the nature of ideological practice.

Althusser's account of ideological practice differentiates it from economic and political practice in a way which makes it autonomous yet also partially determined by them. The notion of ideology as 'false representation', or any kind of representation at all, is rejected. Instead, ideology is used to refer to the lived relation between the individual and the world; as such, it is not 'right' or 'wrong', it simply has certain specific effects. Thus, women and men may or may not live 'as if' they are equal, but either way what is involved is an ideological relation, with the important differentiation being the different effects of those relationships. This means that ideology is not to do with consciousness: 'It is profoundly *unconscious* ... [acting] functionally on men via a process that escapes them' (Althusser, 1965, p. 233). Ideology is also not limited to an abstract world of ideas: it is 'material' in the sense of being embodied in social institutions (marriage, the police and judiciary, etc.) and expressed in objective social forms (language). Ideology does not, therefore, 'determine' experience; rather, it refers to the social axes around which experience becomes organised. To take an example that will be considered in detail later: one of the structural characteristics of our society is its patriarchal organisation, interweaving with its class consitution in a complex but mutually supportive manner. Patriarchy is institutionalised in many ways, one of the most powerful of which is the female domination of child care. This produces certain patterns of interaction in early life and certain structural meanings concerned with the division of the world along gender lines; these meanings are internalised and supply a set of axes around which the developing child's experience becomes organised. The child does not just become conscious of the patriarchal structure of society and confuse it with a 'natural' state of things (false consciousness); instead, patriarchy is experienced as a *principle*, defining a field of possible relationships.

If ideology is not to do with false representation, then it is also universal, in the sense that it will even be present in a socialist society. There is no way in which an individual subject can experience the 'truth' of her/his world in an unmediated fashion, because the conditions of existence never exist in a form available to perception. Instead, they exist as principles in which the individual subject her/himself is constructed; the subject is not some essential, irreducible entity, but is constituted as a subject by the social world. Social relations can never be reduced, as even some Marxist Utopian theories try to do, to intersubjective relations; social structures are of a different order. The individual subject's link with this order is through what Althusser calls an 'imaginary' relationship: 'The imaginary ... consists in the idea that the subject lives its relation to its conditions of existence *as if* it were a subject' (Hirst, 1979, p. 34). This is not another way of talking about illusion: the 'as if' relationship is the reality of the subject, the way in which the world is experienced. The attraction of this account is that it directs attention to the effects of ideological practice, and provides a forum for examining the way the apparently autonomous individual is constructed in the flux of contradictions that have their origin in the social sphere. In the next two chapters psychoanalytic concepts will be employed to spell out the details of how this social construction occurs; the important point here is that we have, at least in outline, a theoretical framework that encompasses the contradictions and oppressions of the social world and the lived experience of the individual.

DISCOURSES AND POWER

In our account of the social world we have emphasised the importance of structural divisions and contradictions, particularly regarding class but also, in the last section, patriarchy. These are basic organising principles that characterise our society, that are articulated in ideology, and that provide the basis for the ideological construction of individuals. But they are rarely experienced in a 'pure' form; rather, there are multitudinous ways of perceiving and articulating relationships that compete for dominance, with the underlying class and gender structures determining which of them are most likely to predominate. Thus an aspect of ideological practice is that a variety of these 'discourses' may coexist in contradiction with one another, some of them being submerged but still supplying a tension which ensures that ideological practice is never experienced as homogeneous and unproblematic. For example, there may be several ways in which sexual orientation as homosexual or heterosexual may be articulated: as an opposition between unnatural and natural, between illness and health, or between repression and liberation, or as a false dichotomy where there is 'in reality' a range of possibilities. Marriage may be an expression of 'romance', an institutionalisation of oppression, a 'sanctity', a fraud. It is not that one cannot think alternative thoughts to those endorsed by the social structures in which one lives; rather, the discourses that dominate, within as well as between people, are likely to be those that can be enforced by the power relations that characterise the social world.

While it may be possible to conceive of a society where human relations are not regulated by laws, it is impossible to imagine them not being organised around discourses. Unless we are to put anything positive about human relations outside politics, this means that discourses must be conceived of as both positive and negative in their effects. To talk about power relations linked to discourses is therefore to do more than refer to a negative imposition of control or oppression by one group or person on another. A different conception of power is implied from that commonly employed, which it is necessary to clarify.

Most political and sociological theories have adopted a monolithic view of power in which lower level organisations are seen merely as serving the ends of higher structures. This negative conception of power sees it as being 'held' by some central authority and employed oppressively to enforce and constrain – indeed, our discussion of the state was along these lines. There are problems with taking this view of certain practices to which it may be applicable and generalising into a theory of all power relationships: it is hard to conceptualise power relationships between individuals (are all individual men acting only in the service of some central, patriarchal authority when they oppress women?) and it carries the discouraging message that the only type of power that exists is oppression. It severely limits the concept of political activity, and so at a practical level is more a recipe for pessimism than a spur to action. This is because it implies that to change anything at one level it is necessary to change the level higher up, ultimately confronting the central structures from which power is considered to emanate. Consequently it appears that there is little point engaging in activity at any level if it is not part of the concurrent revolutionary transformation of the whole social order.

This clearly militates against consideration of the individual and microsocial levels of activity and leads to a simplistic view of complex relationships and institutions. For example, psychiatric hospitals may indeed be instruments of the state that are used to control people, or at least as a substitute for helping them. To make this criticism does not, however, free one from the responsibility for considering what can actually be done when faced with individuals experiencing psychological disturbances. In working this out it might be useful to consider whether psychiatric hospitals also have positive functions that would need to be incorporated into any alternative intervention strategy. However, the overwhelming tendency of socialists to view psychiatric hospitals as *nothing other than* oppressive agencies serving central interests means that no such complex considerations can be entered into. More generally, socialists have often moved from a claim that psychological distress is caused by social conditions to a view that individual treatment which does not attack the social roots of disorder must be normalising and reactionary. In our view this is an asocial approach, failing to recognise the extent to which individualised treatment is itself bound up in sociality and may hence have progressive aspects; once again, it also fails to offer clear guidelines for approaching here-and-now, pre-revolutionary misery, thus vacating the ground for retrogressive, patching-up approaches or worse.

Rather than adopt the centralist or 'top-down' model of power, which, as the illustrations of Chapter 4 demonstrate, can hamper attempts at radical mental health work, we follow Foucault's (1979) conception of power as 'the multiplicity of force relations immanent in the sphere in which they operate and which constitute their own organization' (p. 93). Power is constructed throughout the social sphere, in the relationships which form and fade between individuals, groups and classes; it is not imposed from outside, but is produced in the competition between discourses:

> relations of power are not in superstructural positions, with merely a role of prohibition or accompaniment; they have a directly productive role, wherever they come into play.
>
> (Foucault, 1979, p. 94)

Power also produces resistance – resistances are the 'odd term in relations of power' (p. 96). Yet although 'power comes from everywhere', this does not mean it is formless: there are strategic ways in which power relations become organised in certain interests. Among the swarm of points of power and

resistance that pass through institutions and 'apparatuses',
some order appears:

> it is doubtless the strategic codification of these points of
> resistance that makes a revolution possible, somewhat
> similar to the way in which the state relies on the institu-
> tional integration of power relationships.*
>
> (Foucault, 1979, p. 96)

Power is created at all levels of social organisation, but all
levels are themselves in ideological relations, organised
around the giant structuring principles expressed in economic
and political practices. So among all the points of power and
of resistance, multifarious and subversive as they are, some
pattern takes shape, determining the dominance of some
discourses over others, some interests over others. At all
points struggle can and must occur, for there is no central
authority that can be overturned with the confidence that all
else will follow in its wake, and the power relations that are
strategically codified in institutions and state structures also
exist at the level of inter- and intrapersonal experience. In
thinking about the relation between therapeutic work and
politics the positive functions of power structures as well as
the negative must be considered, for it is the promise behind
the positive aspects as well as the threat behind the negative
that maintains them.

HOSPITALS AND DOCTORS

The account of social structure has necessarily become rather
abstract. In the next two chapters the way in which the
individual becomes constructed in the context of this structure
is explored, with particular reference to psychological distress.
For the remainder of this chapter, the uses of our analysis of
discourse and power will be illustrated and developed in the

---

*There is a danger in this position of turning power into an ahistorical ubiquitous will
o' the wisp; it is unclear whether Foucault's own position, with his rejection of both
psychoanalysis and Marxism, manages to avoid this.

context of two characteristic institutions of mental health practice: psychiatric hospitals and doctors.

The psychiatric hospital

Mental hospitals have a bad reputation. The writings of sociologists such as Goffman and radical psychiatrists such as Laing combined with the cultural liberalism of the 1960s to produce an 'anti-psychiatry' movement to which the long-stay institution was anathema. With this movement came a notion that still dominates left-wing thought on psychiatry, that of psychiatric hospitals as oppressive, controlling, brutalising, inhuman institutions in which the individuality of patients is systematically destroyed by ECT (electroconvulsive therapy) and massive doses of major tranquillisers. Films such as 'One Flew Over the Cuckoo's Nest', a suspicion of psychiatric 'experts', and a glamorisation of madness in the wake of experimentation with drugs such as LSD, all contributed to an image of madness as a poetic escape, or a sane response to an insane world. Correspondingly, the mental hospital became a symbol of the way creative, liberating impulses can be shackled, imprisoned and sealed off from the sanitised world of 'normality' that they threaten to undermine.

The image of being dragged off screaming by men in white coats is one that retains its power, and which is both an element in and a contributor to a fear and fascination with 'madness' that goes back at least as far as the sixteenth century (see Foucault, 1967). It arguably represents the discourse on mental health that still dominates on the left: for instance, the radical London magazine *City Limits* reviewed a November 1983 television programme with the note that 'What's missing from TV's approach to mental illness is the anti-psychiatry input of the 1960s – R.D. Laing, Thomas Szasz, David Cooper. Still, TV always was twenty years behind the times' (*City Limits*, 112, November 1983). The arrogance with which the 'truth' is known by the reviewer reveals not just an ignorance of theoretical developments since the anti-psychiatry movements, but also an unwillingness to consider the detailed realities of psychiatric treatments and mental hospitals. Possession of a discourse that solves the problems of the real world in one sweep can be comforting, but it can also lead away from action through failing to note the alternative discourses that are also available, perhaps also representing parts of 'the truth'. A radical approach cannot start with simplistic givens; it requires a detailed examination of descriptive material. The following is a previously unpublished account by one of the authors of the experience of being a worker in a psychiatric hospital:

Christmas Day On The Wards

It's Christmas day and I'm on my way to the hospital. I wonder why. I'm aware of a sense of obligation, it's something one is supposed to do, though it's not 'expected', and therefore if I do it it will be appreciated by ... who? As a psychologist I'm an outsider, a member of the 'other disciplines' as the nurses call them. To prove I really care (about the nurses? about the patients?) I feel I ought to do things like go in on Christmas day, but feeling forced to do things to prove I'm genuine only makes me feel inauthentic and obscures whatever I might 'really' feel. And then it occurs to me that feelings aren't everything, they need to be used, to be thought about to be helpful, and I've got so bound up with my feelings about coming in that I've never stepped back and asked myself whether it's a good idea. And a good idea for who? For me, for the psychology department, for the hospital, for the patients even? And all these tangles I get into result in my feeling not very much at all, except a kind of emotional grey which I'm dimly aware is the product of so many feelings mixed together that they've ceased to be differentiated: a questionable altruism, guilt, resentment, impatience. I've arrived.

There aren't as many cars in the car park as usual, it's easy to park. There obviously aren't too many administrators and non-nursing professionals around today. There'll be more nurses and porters, the latter needing the overtime, the former needing that and also too often somewhere to be on Christmas day.

The corridors are quiet. They always are actually, except for the sound of brisk professional footsteps and the occasional disturbed patient. Most patients wander around noiselessly, and there are usually a few just hanging around aimlessly, perhaps hoping to scrounge a fag. Today, though, the corridors are empty not only of human activity and voices, but of the bodies that sustain them too.

The first ward I visit is C ward. I won't be working there after Christmas, and have only been there sporadically since the summer. Our departmental reorganisation has meant we're withdrawing what little psychology input there was to C ward, in favour of a ward where more could be done. We're a large hospital department, but we still only have the resources to work on about a quarter of the wards.

The dining area of C ward looks stunning. Christmas decorations and a beautifully laid table: the brilliant white tablecloth, rich red napkins, crackers and wine glasses presaging what is obviously going to be a full-scale Christmas lunch. C ward is well known for the extraordinary amount of effort and care the staff put into making special occasions special. The patients at such times undoubtedly get more lavish treatment than any of the staff would lay on for their own friends or family. That says something about how unexciting and frustrating the everyday work is: getting the patients up at 6.45, encouraging them to dress and wash themselves, calming down Alan who always shouts in the morning, trying to get Jean up in time for breakfast; helping them make their beds, the nurses all the while restraining from doing it themselves even though they could do it in a minute and the patient will take twenty; by which time Fred is stealing Alf's fags and Sam's getting agitated and Jenny's refusing to go to Occupational Therapy, and the students are clamouring to go for their break, and Albert's smiling benignly, insisting he's just off to the Industrial Department when you know that he's so obsessional that it'll take him an hour to get out of his chair, let alone leave the ward.

It happens every morning, but this morning as I wander in at 10 o'clock the atmosphere is different. The patients look smart. They're still spilling ash on their clothes, but their eyes are more animated, their faces more expressive. One or two even say hello and wish me happy Xmas.

C ward is the end of the line. Most of the patients there are over 60, and they wouldn't be there if there was a chance of them leaving hospital. They fit the picture of the classic institutionalised patient: shambling, apathetic, withdrawn, unspontaneous. Most of them have been there for decades. They can still laugh, though, still enjoy themselves, still get angry and moody, it's just that they've settled for their lot, there's no hope and no future and no past that's memorably different to the present, or at least everyone pretends there isn't. That means you don't often see patients look sad because sadness implies an awareness of something that was and is no longer, or at least a recognition that things could have been different to how they are. Of course there is sadness, immense sadness, but it's become a permanent state of affairs, so you don't notice it because there's no background to differentiate it from. It's part of the background against which everything else is perceived, and that's why, paradox- ically, it's most noticeable when the patients aren't sad – you suddenly realise that they were all this time. It's hard to know how real my perception of sadnes is, though. Perhaps it's less disturbing to imagine oneself surrounded by sadness rather than disintegration.

I'm offered a drink which I take and hang around sipping uneasily for the next quarter of an hour. It's uncomfortable because I'm not a nurse, because I'm leaving. The nurses had no say in the decision, nor are they explicitly aware of the reasons for it. 'I'm needed elsewhere', is how one nurse puts it. I'm feeling clumsy, the nurses angry and rejected, but it's not said. On this ward the boundaries between professionals are so tightly maintained for reasons that it's taken me two years to decide I couldn't change, that the main form of com- munication goes on in the form of awkward silences of varying lengths. The jokey, easy going conversations say something, but the gaps between them say a lot more. I feel like I'm handling saying goodbye badly; even that's become part of the job.

It would be dishonest of me to say that I've enjoyed working with them and am sorry to be leaving. I haven't and I'm not. At this moment I just want to get out as quickly as possible. I finish my drink, say I'll drop in some time, wish them all the best and a happy Christmas, make some joke about their having given me such a large drink that I'd be in no state to drive to my family's for lunch, feel guilty that I'm going to be with my family this Christmas and they're not, shake hands and say goodbye.

Walking down the corridor to G ward, I'm aware of a huge sense of relief, and I discover to my surprise that I *am* sad to have left C ward.

G ward is the best rehabilitation ward in the hospital. People leave and cope with being outside, despite having been in hospital sometimes for 40 or 50 years. Although there's presently tension betwen the sister and charge nurse, it's usually a happy ward. Walking on to it you feel that human beings live rather than subsist there.

Sister's not here today, and the atmosphere is lethargic. There isn't the same feeling of a group of people coming together for Christmas that there was on C ward, but it's possibly the more real for that. Some patients have already gone home to relatives for today, one or two more are hanging around waiting to be collected, a mixture of anxiety and eager anticipation on their faces. Today they're going to be part of the world they came from and had all but lost hope of going back to. Although there'll be a big lunch here, too, it'll be a more desultory affair. The nurses have less invested in being there. Many of the nurses on C ward were going to be there all day, despite their duty finishing at 2.30. On G ward the staff have half an eye on the clock because they want to get back to their families. Their home isn't the hospital, and nor is the patients', and it shows.

I'm offered a drink, ask for and get a small one. The charge nurse and a couple of students chat to me in the staff room. They didn't seem to know how to cope with the patients on Christmas day, so seemed glad to have me to talk to and drink with to justify not being with the patients. The consultant was due with his family, then perhaps they could relax. Or get ready to go home. I feel slightly ill at ease because the nurses I know best aren't around, some off for Christmas, some due in on the afternoon shift. The token nature of my visit felt uncomfortably clear. Yet it wasn't a token without meaning. It would be remembered, remarked upon. But what would be remembered would be the fact of my having visited, what was going on now was irrelevant to that, just part of the job.

Part of my job as psychologist to visit, part of their job as nurses to appreciate it. The patients seemed to be the only ones with a free choice as to how to react, though they also had their chosen or allotted roles. It suddenly seemed as if everyone was trying to care and wondering if they did care or whether anyone else did either, or whether they weren't pretending; and it was impossible to sort out who did or didn't care because no-one knew, and everyone did and didn't care and did and didn't know. Everyone so desperate to care and be cared for, to be with other people because even if they weren't the people they really wanted to be with, at least they were there and that was or would have to be enough. It was definitely Christmas.

*   *   *

The first thing that this piece does is oppose the romantic discourse of madness and the 'oppressive' discourse of mental hospitals. The patients' 'madness' is far from glamorous: it is shown to be mundane, often stereotyped, distressing, frustrating, disturbing – anything but an exciting voyage of discovery into the recesses of the human mind. Correspondingly, the staff are far from brutal: they care in their different ways, are themselves in need of company and support; more dependent staff seem to have gravitated to more dependent patients. In some respects, the humanity of the hospital is endorsed: staff make real attempts at caring; the patients, though shambling and apathetic, possess some individuality, have emotions, pasts, in some cases the ability to go home for Christmas. On the other hand, the hints of professional hierarchies, the hollowness of the communication between the psychologist and the nurses, make it apparent that the piece is not dealing with straightforward human relationships; spontaneous emotional expression is heavily inhibited. So there is neither total acceptance of the 'radical' discourse identified earlier, nor total rejection: it is a way of comprehending the hospital's events, but it is not the only one that defines how staff and patients experience the hospital, nor how the psychologist writes about it. Other discourses operate which seem to describe more accurately the 'as if' way in which the author and his characters actually live their experience of the hospital. The most powerful of these appears to be one balanced on a dimension of 'outside versus inside'.

The division between the hospital and the outside world appears as a dominant image in many discourses on 'mental illness', including both the radical view of mental-hospital-as-prison and the traditional 'asylum' concept. This notion can be questioned in many ways. Although it is true that large psychiatric hospitals tend to be outside urban connurbations, they are also large employers. In addition, given that around 10 per cent of the population spend some time within a psychiatric hospital during their life, the sense in which they are literally outside of everyday life is questionable. 'Outsided' might be a better way of putting it: one ideological relation is that people live 'as if' madness and mental hospitals were outside their experience, and this may apply as much to staff in a hospital as to the somewhat theoretical 'naive' member of the general public.

The author addresses the outside-inside discourse in a number of ways. First, by choosing Christmas day he links life in the hospital with life outside, as he does more ambiguously by describing himself as an outsider going into the hospital and the patients waiting to go home for the day. The distinction between outsiders and insiders is contained in a range of references, with at one end the complete outsiders (the author's parents, the patients' relatives) in the middle the various hospital workers and groups of nurses, and at the other end the patients who are 'inside' forever and are not going home. On the one hand the notion of the hospital as the 'place', cut off from the outside world, is rejected in favour of a more subtle gradation of inside and out; on the other hand it is endorsed in that both the author and the hospital are preoccupied with defining the inside-outside relationship. Importantly, two separate discourses are being referred to throughout this discussion, their entanglement making their ideological consequences more pervasive. Both use the inside-outside axis, but differently. One refers to insiders as people within the hospital – predominantly staff who face the reality of mentally ill patients, but also (the 'asylum' discourse) patients facing the 'outside' world with trepidation. The effect of this discourse is to produce the mental hospital as a special place, probably misunderstood by the ignorant world, an island of reality ('in-the-know') whose walls are defensive ones. The other inside-outside discourse places the hospital as 'outside' – outside the community, a place of separateness, strangeness and isolation. As will be discussed in Chapter 6, this discourse also produces an ideologically powerful notion of the 'community' as a unified, caring place, to which one might want psychiatric patients to return; that such a harmonious, integrated community is a fantasy does not lessen its power.

This discussion of the differences that lie even within the apparently homogeneous 'inside-outside' distinction demonstrates the dangers of ignoring the details of ideological relations, the precise way in which different discourses coexist and compete for dominance in the 'as if' relationships that we make with the social world. The most significant of these dangers is that the simplistic adoption of one discourse as the only 'true' one will render impossible the task of unravelling the complexities of people's experiences of themselves and others. This is not to argue that some views of the world are not better than others: we have already articulated our conception of how the social world is 'really' constituted, in terms of economic, political and ideological practice. Rather, we are arguing against tendencies to reduce the complexity of the real world to simple generalities, most of which rely on the 'top-down' model of power criticised earlier. Thus the 'asylum' discourse would view psychiatric hospitals only as places of refuge ('if you closed them down, how would these poor people cope?'); 'medical' discourse views them as places of treatment for illness; the dominant radical discourse views them simply as oppressive state structures. Analysis of the detail of psychiatric hospital experiences throws up a series of questions that are not answerable in these terms. For example, the piece above suggests that psychiatric hospitals do not entirely smash individuality, do leave patients capable of feeling emotions, and do contain caring and warm staff. On the other hand, normal working days are frustrating and emotionally flat, dependency is generated in patients and staff alike, communications are suspicious and impoverished, hierarchies operate pervasively. How do all these things come about, whose interests do they serve, how are they maintained, what might replace them? The reason why these questions are not easily answered is that the features they identify as being in need of change have both positive and negative functions for staff and patients – they are not *simply* the product of extrinsic power relations. For example, the rigid hierarchies and practices that often characterise long-stay institutions are not just ways of dehumanising patients, but are also expressions of the difficulties that staff have in containing and handling extreme emotions (Menzies, 1960). At the same time they are manifestations of the vested interests of the different professions. Again, emotional flatness may well be experienced by all concerned as preferable to florid psychosis, and this is reflected by the gravitation of staff to wards that 'fit' their own needs; in this way, flatness may be dehumanising at the same time as providing important protection for staff and patients alike.

It is not the case that the 'positive' elements described above in themselves justify the power relations that operate in places such as psychiatric hospitals. Rather, they have to be comprehended if an intervention is to change things, instead of producing a new version of the same underlying state of affairs. In the analysis of the institutions of mental health care, awareness of the complexity of power relations, the ways in which obviously negative structures can be maintained by fulfilling certain real needs, and an account of the ideological relations that mediate the experiences that people have of one another, are all essential elements, without which no radical practice can be produced. In the next section we argue that the same imperative applies to the analysis of the commonest image of health care, the doctor–patient relationship.

Doctors and psychiatrists

The doctor–patient relationship is a complex one. Most obviously, it consists in what goes on in the consulting room, in 'going to the doctor's' – the request for diagnosis, treatment, prescription or reassurance. Although the image of the family doctor has become somewhat tarnished in recent years, there remains a dominant discourse which has clear and powerful characteristics. In its most extreme form, the family doctor is almost a religious figure, not just with respect to her/his curative powers, but in the notion of the benevolent, omniscient, patriarchal expert who tends for 'his' patients and understands not just their physical health, but also their family history, everyday troubles and worries. This is the image supported by the medical profession, but also by conservative politics of various shades, which use it as one prop for the romance of the traditional, homogeneous 'community' – the doctor, the policeman and the vicar acting to protect and nurture their flock. While most people know this image of the doctor to be grossly idealised, that their experience is often of incompetence or insincerity on the part of their family doctor, and that other images also exist (the white-coated hospital doctor being a significant one), the romantic image produces an idealisation which affects the experiences of doctors and patients and consequently has a place in the social world. For example, the disillusionment commonly felt with doctors and medical attitudes is often based on their failure to conform to the idealised model, the 'implicit image' with which one confronts the reality of one's doctor. It may therefore be useful to consider in more detail some of the elements that go to make up this image.

The doctor is above all a possessor of knowledge, an expert. This means not only that s/he possesses awesome powers of judgement but that mere lay people have no right to challenge medical opinions – or even to ask for explanations of the impenetrable jargon which doctors have in common with other state bureaucrats. The reverse side to this expertise is therefore the non-expert's inadequacy and ignorance. Technological society is of course full of experts of various kinds, but what makes the doctor unusual is that the object of her/his knowledge is the person consulting her/him. This sets up a relationship that is bound to be prone to all kinds of distortion, for the patient must give up power in order to be helped: it is only by relinquishing one's privacy, of both body and mind, that the patient can hope to receive adequate treatment. The literal and metaphorical stripping of the patient's protective clothing must arouse anxieties in patients of being attacked or humiliated (hence the 'by the way, doctor' phenomenon where patients mention the issues that are worrying them just as they are leaving) and may confirm the doctor's fantasy of being able to control or dominate others. In the light of this, it is understandable that the concept of the doctor who is 'part of the family' should be so appealing. The power structure of the doctor–patient relationship is accentuated by what Foucault (1973) has called the 'medical gaze', the adoption of a critical, 'objective', distanced way of regarding patients and their illnesses. This stance involves a mistrust of personal emotional responses, a rejection of the importance of 'understanding' as opposed to 'knowing'. In this image the doctor is male, and there is a marked contrast between the way the doctor looks into the patient, attempting to penetrate her/him in order to get at the truth of the illness, and the corresponding look of the (female) nurse, which is concerned with understanding and caring, looking *after* rather than *into*. It also involves caring for the patient, rather than treating the illness.

The dialogue between doctor and patient is thus an odd one, containing social and subjective functions that are central to the way people perceive and try to understand their experience. These link with certain political issues – that is, they are all important elements in ideological practice. For example, the elements in the doctor–patient relationship described lead people to regard their suffering, their physical and psychological 'symptoms' as apart from themselves and their environment, and consequently promote a passive attitude towards help. In this way both the social causation of illness and the processes involved in being ill are split off from a person's experience, and illness becomes something that just happens, takes its course and hopefully goes away, without any inner or outer complexity. In being inexpert about their illnesses, people become inexpert about themselves.

In a sense, a reason why people have psychological symptoms is often precisely that they have split off parts of themselves as unmanageable, and this process would not necessarily be modified by their having a different attitude to doctors. Nevertheless, the strength with which people internalise notions of what feelings are or are not permissible, what feelings are dangerous or disturbing, means that it would be wrong to underestimate the importance of the 'doctor's' as a place, both actual and as an image, where painful feelings and experiences can be taken. This discourages people from using their own practical and emotional resources to deal with distress, or to effect changes in the environment. Thus political issues become reduced to individual, private matters that must be dealt with by an expert. So, for example, depressed women are doled out tranquillisers *en masse* to soothe the anxiety generated by the impossible burden of having to care for husbands and children with little emotional support and with no encouragement to perceive their difficulties as a product of the appalling social provision for childcare and the isolation of young mothers (Brown and Harris, 1978). The way in which people come to see certain aspects of themselves as needing treatment, thereby turning themselves into 'cases', parallels the 'breakdown' model adopted by mental health workers, which implies that once the breakdown is remedied everything can return to some notional condition of smooth functioning. The romantic discourse surrounding the family doctor therefore contributes to the conformist idea that the natural state of society is to run smoothly, that breakdowns are individual affairs, to be treated while leaving the social fabric untouched. This is particularly the case with 'mental illness', where the symptoms are less tangible, and where the everyday terminology of 'nervous breakdown' is used indiscriminately to cover a multiplicity of feelings, causes and effects.

Related to the way in which the romantic discourse of the doctor defines for people aspects of their conceptions of themselves is a broader ideological role that includes the propagation of a certain image of family life and a denial of the relevance of gender, race, class and politics to people's lives. Paradoxically, this involves both a focus on individuality and a weakening of the power of individuals to control and define their experiences. Politics is denied in the sense that illnesses are located inside individuals, where they are an alien presence – hence there is nothing that the individual can do about them except trust in the doctor's expertise. But the discourse of the hospital doctor goes even further than this, to assert the dominance of a particular mode of social functioning and to replicate it in the actual practice of medicine, even more in hospitals than in the family doctor's surgery. This mode is that of the family, the idealised family of ideological practice where father exercises power and embodies the law, and mothers are caring and supportive, staying at home to look after the children. The analogy between the professional roles of doctors and nurses and the traditional male and female roles is very striking. Doctors possess knowledge and power, they lay down the law ('prescribe'), they are rarely present – just as fathers go out to work but rule the home in their absence and the threat of their presence. Nurses care and understand, are always stuck on the ward on low pay with neither the power to change their position nor the 'qualifications' for their opinions to be noted or their work appreciated – just as the housewife is left at home doing unappreciated work, holding the baby. It is no accident that the medical profession's basic structure reflects that of the family, with patients treated as children, in need of looking after, with no adult understanding of their predicament, or of what is best for them. The 'medical model' in this context is much more than just a theory of mental illness; it is also a solidly embedded and defended power structure with enormous material effects, one of these being the reproduction of conformist notions of care and family life with their attendant sexual division of knowledge, labour and power.

Up to this point, the ideological status of the ordinary doctor has been examined, with particular attention to the effectiveness of the dominant discourses in perpetuating individualistic and conformist notions of normality. 'Normality' is represented as a smoothly functioning social arena modelled on conventional family life, with breakdowns being aberrations due to the unfortunate, or sometimes blameworthy, infection of individuals with alien substances. This analysis applies equally to many discourses surrounding those doctors who become psychiatrists, but with some important modifications. The main additional point is that (contrary to attitudes *within* the medical profession) psychiatrists usually have attributed to them even greater and more specialised wisdom and insight, particularly in relation to 'deep' meanings and processes, an ability to read people's minds better than the people themselves. This notion is quite at odds with psychiatric training, which until recently has almost totally ignored meanings and mental processes in favour of the mastery of systems for the formal classification of symptoms. It presumably derives historically from the way psychoanalysis has been assimilated within popular culture to reinforce the perception of psychiatrists as possessors of magical expertise in the arena of deep meanings, an ironic association given that psychoanalysis presents a thoroughgoing critique of traditional psychiatry's claims to knowledge and understanding. Nevertheless, the misconception persists, and patients frequently expect that seeing a psychiatrist will involve lying on a couch and exploring their past experiences. While many psychiatrists are virulently anti-psychoanalytic, it cannot be said that they go out of their way to dispel the idea that they possess the abilities ascribed to them. This merger of the prestige of the doctor and the mystery of psychoanalysis produces a discourse of 'the psychiatrist' that endorses the power of experts to 'read one's mind' and which further alienates people from ownership of their own emotions and experiences.

In addition to the consequences of these discourses for wider ideological practice (individualism, conformism, the power of 'expertise'), they also affect the supposedly therapeutic interaction between psychiatrist and patient. It is a common experience for all mental health workers to be told by their clients that they have never been able to talk to anyone as they are doing with them. While this may be true, reflecting the poverty of the client's other relationships, it is also true that people easily believe that they are being understood in some penetrating, mysterious way, when in fact all that has happened is that they have been asked a few simple questions about themselves. This both flatters the worker's narcissism and makes for passive, easily managed clients, but it has nothing to do with helping people make sense of their own experience and much to do with further alienating them from their own capacity to think and comprehend, as well as from the 'inexpert' but genuine responsiveness of those around them to their suffering. This is not to say that people are always capable of dealing with their own or each other's distress, nor that it is anything but good to have confidence in someone else's ability to help; on the contrary, however hard it has to be struggled for on both sides, no therapeutic interaction can take place without that confidence. On the other hand, there is a distinction to be made between healthy trust and blind faith.

A doctor–patient dialogue in which the doctor is invested with absolute authority and adopts a position of certainty with respect to the patient's symptoms, reflects a mutual lack of faith in the capacity for suffering to be borne: the patient gives it to the doctor (an 'it' that has to be split off) and the doctor treats, manages or controls it, again holding it at arm's length rather than experiencing it. Gear, Hill and Liendo (1981) have suggested that the power relations present in this interchange have a sado-masochistic structure, in which the doctor is master, the patient slave. Each needs the other, each exists only in relation to the other: the power of the doctor depends in important ways on the recognition that s/he receives from the patient-slave. The situation is not simply a matter of the doctor 'having' power over the patient, for, ironically, 'in fact' he hasn't that power at all, but there is a subtle collusion that goes on in the interests of both parties, and in the wider interests of the ideological order. Since there is a shared but unacknowledged belief that the 'problem' cannot be understood or tolerated, it comes to be in the interests of the patient to maintain the doctor's expertness in order to perpetuate the split that has been introduced into her/his experience (without an expert doctor, the pain might have to be absorbed into the patient's self). Correspondingly, it is in the doctor's interest to do likewise, by pretending s/he understands, whether or not that is the case – otherwise the 'master' position will be lost, and the doctor as well as the patient will have to absorb the pain of the patient's distress. Thus it is that a supposedly therapeutic relationship, dealing with a person's most intimate feelings, can become a ritualis-tic, contentless acting out, having the sole functions of reassur-ing the patient that s/he is being a good patient, and the doctor that s/he is a good therapist. This kind of narcissistic enterprise perpetuates the symbolism of cure and hope in-vested in the doctor ('Is there any hope, doctor? – the soap-opera cliché as a symbol of dependency), once again enhancing political passivity and denying the potential for more meaningful experiences of care.

It is important to stress that nothing we have said constitutes a *personal* criticism of any individual doctor or psychiatrist, nor do we wish to deny the benefits of medicine or the relief from suffering afforded by psychiatry. Obviously there are good and bad doctors and psychiatrists, just like everyone else. Our point is that irrespective of the personal merits of individual practitioners or its positive or negative effects in relation to a particular patient, the doctor–patient relationship will be organised around the discourses described. These discourses are perpetuated in a number of ways, ranging from the most obvious vested interests to the more subtle support derived from the needs of people in distress (e.g. for hope). Their net effect is to deter people from paying sufficient attention either to their inner experiences or to the world in which they live, the context and in large part the cause of their unhappiness. They thereby contribute not only to the creation of a psychiatrist–patient relationship which is often therapeutic only in name, but also to the 'emotional scarcity' and political apathy that is increasingly characteristic of everyday life. This function in turn has its place in the reproduction of power relations, such as those between women and men and between state and citizen, which are tied into the structural contradictions of contemporary society. In mental health, as in other spheres of practice, these power relations are revealed in the interactions between people, as well as in the broader social context.

POWER

The examples of psychiatric hospitals and doctors/psychiatrists explored above demonstrate the complex interweaving of power relations that characterise the mental health arena. At its simplest, because of the influence of the major structuring principles (class, gender, race) in contemporary society, the discourses that dominate mental health can be said to serve the interests of late capitalism. For example, the 'outsidedness' of the psychiatric hospital contributes towards the construction of a myth of the 'natural' community as a cohesive, supportive unit; this myth legitimises state interventions that have the effect of placing the burden for care of psychologically disturbed people on their (female) relatives (see Chapter 6 for a more detailed discussion of the links between 'family' and 'community' discourse). The discourses on doctors as, on the one hand, family confessors and, on the other, technological experts reinforce hierarchical and sexist divisions of labour and knowledge and also produce a split between the individual's experience of pain or distress and the social context that surrounds and infiltrates it. Both these ideological enterprises reduce the possibilities for self-control, dissent and collective struggle by presenting a vision of the social world as harmonious, disrupted only by individual breakdowns, and by perpetrating a reduction of social distress to the realm of the natural or biological, where the appropriate mode of 'treatment' is claimed to be the technological manipulation of individuals. Thus medicine is consumed instead of action being taken; questions surrounding the massive incidence of distress and disturbance in society are transformed into arguments over the adequacy of resources for 'treatment'.

Both the examples presented above show that this analysis of power in terms of the interests served by ideological discourse is not the whole story. If one explores the interactions between the people who fill the roles of 'doctor', 'nurse' and 'patient', it becomes clear that one cannot talk strictly of any individual, group or institution 'having' power, for power cannot be located solely at a central point that needs to be dismantled. Rather, power is generated in the structure within which relationships take place, and every aspect of the structure can be seen to possess positive and negative functions. This does not mean that one cannot ask what could be improved or removed altogether, but it does make problematic some overall judgement such as that psychiatric hospitals are 'bad things'. On the other hand, it is not simply a matter of identifying the 'real' needs that people have and then constructing the best possible institutions to meet them, for these 'needs' are themselves generated and mediated by social structures – that is, no straightforward distinction between an individual's subjective experience and the objective factors that allegedly determine it can be maintained. For example, the 'personal' encounters between (in the psychiatric hospital example) the psychologist and the nurses, their ways of communicating, the emotions that are engendered, can all be seen to be mediated by the institutional setting, and this would be true even if the interactions were of a more desirable kind. Subjective experience cannot be separated from the communications surrounding it, which in turn are as much part of the structure generating these communications as they are utterances 'belonging to' individuals. Even more apparently 'objective' features of the institution, such as strict hierarchies, were seen in the example to have subjective functions which to some extent maintain them. Similarly, to analyse the structure of the doctor–patient relationship as above is not to reduce that relationship and the determinants of its power to the intersubjective qualities that characterise it, although it is to stress the existence of an intersubjective 'underside' to relations that have economic, cultural and other objective determinations too.

The points made above constitute a criticism both of orthodox political and psychoanalytic theory, the former for its simplistic conception of power relations and its correlative neglect of human relationships, the latter for its lack of acknowledgement that therapeutic relationships occur in a context determined by more than a pure, unmediated contact between two people, the patient and the analyst. Although the analytic setting, with its very strict boundaries of time and place, claims to produce a 'pure' contact so that the patient's unconscious fantasies can be revealed, this ignores the way people's experience is continually being influenced by relations which, while not unconscious in the analytic sense, might nevertheless be beyond the conscious access of the patient because they provide the structure in which conscious experience takes place. For example, before the advent of feminism the oppression of women by men was largely not an accessible fact of conscious experience because it was (and still is) structural to the experience of both sexes. Becoming aware of one's oppressiveness or oppression does involve a restructuring of consciousness, but this is distinct from the 'making the unconscious conscious' of the psychoanalytic process.

This last distinction between, as it were, the 'ideological unconscious' and the psychoanalytic unconscious is crucial in avoiding the reduction of the political to the personal or the personal to the political in any simple sense. As well as being a criticism of orthodox psychoanalysis, it is a rejection of those political movements that regard 'the unconscious' simply as internalised oppression. Instead, ideology is comprehended as a structuring principle: it is not that in some liberated society there would be no unconscious (because of the free play of desires in the unmediated interpersonal encounters of socialist Utopia), but that the unconscious would be structured around different axes from those present under capitalism, patriarchy and racism. 'As if' relations always describe how individuals live in the social world, for there is no means by which the individual can step outside the system that constructs her/him in order to form an unmediated relationship with it. Socialist struggle, in this respect, is concerned with changing the content of the 'as if', so that the relationships engendered by it are more equal, less divisive and oppressive.

Because of the complexity of the links between social structures, ideological practice and unconscious feelings, the link between politics and therapy is multiply determined and not reducible to a political line or slogan such as 'the personal is political'. Clearly, for both therapeutic and political practice the ultimate yardstick will be the quality of human relationship that a particular therapy or political system produces: socialism is an attractive political goal because it holds out the promise of more equal, open and fulfilled human relationships than those present under other systems. However, there is also a tension between political and therapeutic practice. For example, as noted earlier, the diversion of a large section of the radicalised middle classes into the helping professions must be seen partly as a neutralisation of their potential for radical political action, irrespective of how beneficial the particular relationships they form may be. Or again, the manner in which psychoanalytic treatment is available almost solely to wealthy people calls into question all claims concerning its revolutionary potential. On the other hand, the concern of political activists only with economic and political practice has meant that many people have become alienated from political struggle because it appears to neglect the details of their personal, emotional experiences. It is here that mental health practice is so provocative, revealing that it is not sufficient simply to place together two givens, the 'personal' and the 'political'. As has been argued throughout this chapter, the two arenas of discourse interpenetrate one another, with mental health practice being significant in the reproduction and modification of both. Close analysis of the ideological practice inscribed in mental health reveals the way in which power relations operate as more than a set of negative extrinsic factors or a diffuse set of intra- and interpersonal motivations. It also shows how 'subjective experience' is always a partial product of, but not reducible to, objective factors and therefore that power relations are operative in all therapeutic encounters, and that the discourses that surround therapeutic activity have important ideological and hence material consequences. All this must be taken into account in developing a politically radical mental health practice: slogans act as important rallying cries, but can become counterproductive if they prevent analysis of the details of action. It is in the exploration of this detail, the uncovering of the various discourses that are present in all mental health encounters, that the seeds of a restructured practice can be found. It is with this justification that the central section of this book is devoted to analyses of examples of therapeutic work.

Finally, although the terms 'personal' and 'emotional' experience have been used several times in this chapter, it is worth considering the political significance of 'feelings'. When a person's politics are discussed, their feelings are usually ignored – 'feelings' are not part of the general image of 'being political'. Rather, it is their ideas that are prioritised, their more or less thought-out preconceptions, prejudices and opinions are taken as indicators of their political position. Obviously, people's ideas are important, but two people can have the same ideas and yet be worlds apart in their feelings and practice. Without having some understanding of the significance of this it is easy to neglect the fact that what people feel is not just 'personal', but is as substantial and influential as what they think. The issue is not whether people's feelings are 'valid' or acceptable, but whether they can be given proper consideration in the way political activity is formulated. Feelings may not be any more tangible than ideas, but they are also no less objective or material. As women have repeatedly told men, the task of taking seriously what people feel is a major project, involving far more than the addition of an extra factor to the equation. To begin with, it requires the toleration of a degree of uncertainty that may be alien to the impassioned political activist. Second, it requires attention to the detail of one's own experience as well as that of others, and therefore the toleration of painful and disturbing feelings. Third, it requires an understanding of mental health and psychological disturbance that does justice to the idiosyncrasies of an individual's experience, at the same time as being able to link the complex and contradictory social construction that each individual is, with the social institutions and power relations of which everyone is a part and a product. What such an understanding might consist of is the subject of Chapters 2 and 3.

2
The Social Construction of the Individual

This chapter introduces the concepts upon which our approach to mental health is based. We argue that theories of individuality have often side-stepped important issues by assuming the existence of a human essence which dictates development, and which constitutes the core of the self. By this 'essentialist' tactic they lose the capacity to explain the complexity of subjective experience, and they separate individuals off from the social world in which they are embedded. The result is a resort to biological predisposition as the primary explanatory concept, one that ignores the need for an account of how human beings enter a world of meaning and symbolic activity. We outline a version of psychoanalysis that avoids these essentialist predicates and permits theorisation of the *social* construction of the individual – the way in which social factors enter into psychological development from earliest childhood.

THE INDIVIDUAL

The conventional view of individuality is that it is based on an inherited set of attributes that we are born with and that both distinguish us from others and define who we are at root. This is an 'essentialist' position in that it is founded on the notion that people have independent and original 'selves' that are not constructed by the social system in which they emerge. Individual existence predates social experience and, however susceptible it may be to social influence, is in essence unmodifiable: you cannot change human nature as a whole, nor can you change that which makes every individual not only human, but different from other humans. Concepts of 'human nature' are intimately tied up with this view that we possess basic, unchangeable, internal characteristics. Individuals are seen as being similar to one another in being 'essentially' aggressive, competitive, nurturant or whatever, but vary quantitatively in pre-given qualities – some are more talented, brighter, more emotional; women are more dependent, men more aggressive and achieving. In this respect, biology is destiny: an individual's 'self' is something s/he brings into the world, the product of heredity or more general evolutionary forces, determining the shape and character of the growing child's interactions with the outside world. How s/he gets on is determined by the self's properties – its character, intelligence, personality or level of creativity. Correspondingly, society is itself made up of these independent, free selves which are essentially separate but interact to form social collectives, free enterprise rewarding those 'cut out' to succeed. On this view there are no 'social forces'; society is equivalent to the summed psychology of individuals.

Although this view of human nature emphasises the separateness of each person from others, it is not usually so crude as to suggest that individuals have no contact with one another or are uninfluenced by external events: clearly, individuals are greatly affected by social phenomena. The point is, however, that these influences are taken as external, affecting individuals but not forming them. This assumption is clearly manifested in psychological accounts of the 'integration' of children into society.

Usually, the child's individual essence is assumed to exist from the start of life – this is what defines her/him as human – so the process of socialisation is one in which this primitive but already whole being learns the rules and controls that make behaviour socially acceptable. In Llewellyn and Kelly's words,

> Psychology sees it as possible and logical to talk about the human individual as an autonomous unit which in some circumstances may be influenced by social factors.
>
> (Llewellyn and Kelly, 1980, p. 407)

According to most theories, children experience these social factors through reinforcement (rewards and punishments contingent upon behaviour) or models whom they imitate or 'identify' with. For example, it is argued that they learn language through discovering which words, when attached to objects or intentions, communicate accurately with adults; they may discover sex roles through conscious-shaping experiences with pink and blue, dolls and guns. Recent theories have recognised the need to postulate something more active within the child to explain how these experiences have their effects, as the notion that there is an automatic link between environmental events and individual behaviour is tenable only in very restricted cases, mostly concerned with physiological responses. The most convincing adaptation of traditional theories is to add a 'cognitive' mediating component, such that, for instance, the child is thought to make judgements or predictions about the world which s/he then assesses against experience. For example, a child makes some kind of plausible hypothesis about the implications of its early recognition of itself as female or male, and tests this out by observations of, and interactions with, the people around it. Gradually, the hypotheses become more and more refined, until the 'grammar' of adult existence has been learned.

This view of socialisation plausibly describes the acquisition of many skills and attitudes, particularly since the addition of a cognitive component removes the excessively passive flavour of traditional behaviourist theories. It has major flaws, however. First, it is extremely individualistic, explaining the development of each child in terms only of her/his own experiences, with no reference to the larger social structures within which these experiences take place. The only space that is given to structural factors is that they can be hypothesised to influence the behaviour of socialising agents: for example, boys might become violent because their fathers are violent because they live in a society which valorises male violence. Similarities between people are explained solely by similarities in their experiences; differences between people can therefore only be explained by appeal to genetically endowed characteristics if their environments are perceived as similar. These theories are thus *microsocial*, in that they concentrate on the immediate experiences of the child, and are restricted in explanatory power to situations in which the child's learning is a direct response to the more or less intended acts of her/his caretakers. As there is little consideration of socially pervasive influences, notably ideology, there is no non-biologistic way of explaining why a child might learn things differently from the teachings of adults (for example, why a child may be sex-typed despite the most enthusiastic of non-sexist rearings), or why the intellectual and emotional responses of children brought up in widely differing settings might be remarkably akin.

A second, related limitation operates in a different direction. Most theories take for granted the existence of a consciousness that directs the activities of the child, and deal principally with phenomena that can safely be incorporated into conscious experience. This means that while they may explain quite well how certain skills are learned, they are impoverished in their explanations of *subjective* development – emotions, desires, fantasies, a sense of self. The meanings that people create for themselves, the parts of their existence which seem most central, are left unaccounted for because they are assumed at the start: a child might act in a certain manner because of its desires, with no discussion of how those desires originate. Put more strongly, while traditional theories might reasonably explain certain types of behaviour, they cannot effectively explain experience, the subjective sources of, and responses to, external and internal events. The essence of the individual, what defines her/him for what s/he is, is assumed as pre-existent and hence pre-social, rather than described and explained in developmental terms.

The position characterised here is not just the simple 'genes determine behaviour' argument of some physiological theorists, nor the fashionable sub-discipline of 'sociobiology' which makes explicit claims that human social behaviour is determined by biological factors. All theories of the individual which do not explicitly deal with the social construction of individuality are essentialist, no matter what weight they place on socialisation processes. For example, this is the case with the theory which apparently most emphasises the effects of the environment on human behaviour, namely behaviourism. Seemingly an extreme form of environmentalism, stating that all behaviour is learned and predictable from past and present environmental conditions and (at least in the account put forward by Skinner, 1971) that 'free will' is an empty concept, behaviourism finds itself faced with the problem of explaining consistent individual differences in behaviour under apparently similar circumstances, and is forced to explain them in terms of genetically inherited characteristics. Hence the apparent contradiction that avowed behaviourists concern themselves predominantly with physiological events and genetic hypotheses to explain differences in personality and intelligence (see, for instance, Eysenck's work).

Most liberal and 'radical' approaches to individuality are unfortunately also founded in essentialism. For example, the influential movement in psychology towards explanations of behaviour in terms of 'interactions' between the 'person' and the 'situation' does not take us very far, as for interaction to take place there must already be integrated individuals. 'Interactionism leaves its own constituents unexamined and preserves the dualities at the heart of the interaction' (Riley, 1978, p. 79). Similar criticisms, that 'individual' and 'society' are left as unanalysable and separate entities, can be applied to other, apparently more radical, theories. For example, two favourites of the left, Reich and Laing, both resort to theoretical constructs revolving around an underlying personal wholeness which has been repressed or distorted by the bad world outside. Reich's account of the effects of sexual repression and Laing's working out of the notion of 'ontological insecurity' are both essentialist, the former because it supposes an underlying individuality that could achieve fulfilment through sexual activity if repressive controls were removed; the latter because it supposes a whole and integrated ego into which splits are introduced by painful experiences (see Mitchell, 1974, for a full account; Laing's theories are discussed again in Chapter 3). Finally, sociological accounts fit this category, limiting their social psychological concepts to simple notions of 'roles' or 'conditioning'.

The essentialist tendency, viewing the self as pre-existent, affected by society but constructed outside it, is thus widespread, often unacknowledged but generally functioning as the 'common-sense' basis for attempts to understand human psychology. This widespreadness is itself a ground for suspicion: if there is a general message that Marxist notions of ideology have communicated clearly it is that common-sense is often false consciousness, the 'half-truths of a deceitful society' (Jacoby, 1975). Certainly, individualism is an historically determined conception, linked with the rise of capitalism and the change of organisation from social tradition to the selling of individual labour power. Previously, individuals were viewed as social in their nature (their essence), the most common image being that of the biological organism 'whose parts (individuals) were constituted only in relation to the whole. Physical individuals were the bearers or occupiers of pre-given social positions and characteristics, rather than their creators' (Llewellyn and Kelly, 1980, p. 407). Concepts of individual morality and 'soul' present in Christianity provide an older basis for western essentialism, merging with capitalist notions of freedom and personal responsibility to create a common-sense tied to a particular mode of social organisation. That this is culturally as well as historically relative is clear from examples of societies in which individuals are designated by their role and may change their 'individual' identity according to their seniority or maturity (see Hirst and Woolley, 1982, p. 119). However, it is not because essentialist theories are historically determined but because they are inadequate that we take issue with them. They cannot meet the demand for an account of individuality that explores the way in which the construction of the self takes place during development, because the self is assumed, allocated a position as a rational and self-directing cipher, determined in its attributes from the moment of conception. Politics and power relations remain external to the individual because there is no theory of individuality – social forces simply modify the way in which one's essential characteristics are expressed. Whether one holds that society enables 'human nature' to flourish or that society crushes it, this presents great difficulties for understanding either personal distress or social injustice, and taken to its extreme makes change inconceivable. Individuals cannot change because their nature is pre-determined; society cannot change because it is made up of these unmodifiable selves in free contact, which is why society reflects 'natural' characteristics such as greed, self-interest or competitiveness. Social injustice is thus reducible to a reflection of human nature. Individual distress cannot be explained except as the necessary consequence of the world that individuals have created for themselves.

This account of the implications of essentialist theory is admittedly extreme, but reveals the conformist basis of such theories, a conformism that is eventually articulated in all theories which share its premises. Thus, while it is not surprising to discover the biological determinism underlying the behaviourism of such reactionary psychologists as Eysenck, many people who have admired the anti-psychiatric polemic of authors such as Szasz and Laing have been shocked to encounter their conformism, expressed by the former in advocacy of free enterprise for mental health care, and by the latter in mysticism (see Sedgwick, 1982, for a more detailed account of these tendencies). Yet the conformism is an integral part of the theories, however obscured by more attractive features. For Szasz, psychiatry is a means of control over individual liberty and personal choice: all conducts are consciously chosen, so one can only be bad, not mad. For Laing, the inner essence of the individual is primordially good and whole, and society only distorts or represses it. The solution is consequently not social change, but escape to the 'alpha and omega' of it all, the inner self.

The assumption of a universal human nature ignores the multiplicity of forms of personal and social expression that determine the content of thoughts, feelings and behaviours. For example, sexual desires are not just the consequences of physiological states or conscious choice, but take place in a system of discourses that develops a certain aim, shape and content for desire, as well as varying the conditions of repression – the only role for society that essentialist theories would allow (Foucault, 1979). Thus the myth of a pre-given biological sexuality obscures the ways heterosexuality is bound to the specific conditions of social existence and is expressed in particular 'surfaces of emergence' (Foucault, 1973); far from being a truth of human nature, the discourse of 'natural' heterosexuality itself plays a part in the construction of heterosexual relations. The social formation of sexual desire has even been neglected until recently in feminist literature (Segal, 1983). Personal hopes, intentions and meanings all arise in a context of social structures that pre-date the individual, and take their particular form within these structures. Failure to acknowledge this misses both the political nature of psychological development and the complexity of human experience. In her chapter for Cartledge and Ryan's (1983) book *Sex and Love*, Lynne Segal gives an example of this limitation. Taking issue with feminist advice on sexuality, which has assumed an ability to take conscious control over one's sexual feelings, Segal describes her own masochistic fantasies and the ways in which they are entwined not just with evident social processes, but also with the unconscious internalisation of those processes. Her message is twofold: first, that sexual desire cannot be manipulated for it is unconsciously structured and hence recalcitrant. More centrally for our own concerns, Segal criticises romanticised notions of female sexuality as 'naturally joyful [and] self-nourishing' (p. 40), arguing that they obscure the reality of sexual experience, which is both less idyllic and more complex. Particular varieties of sexual desire and fantasy are no more 'basic' than are particular manifestations of aggressiveness: social structuring takes place in all psychological arenas, and it is only through recognition of this that the complications of personal experience can be made intelligible. Sociologising and psychologising are both reductively simplistic; to adapt Segal's words, our feelings are 'buried inside us as well as reflected in the social world which shaped them to begin with' (p. 43).

Consider another example. A young female patient was referred for help because of an obsessive fear that she would catch fire or explode. There were some elements to her problem that could be explained reductively. For instance, her family generally devalued her in favour of a younger brother, and the only way she could gain attention was through adoption of extravagant symptoms. This was not the whole explanation, however, for although she was aware of her exclusion from her family, her experience of her symptoms was of something outside her control, that could not be removed by a conscious decision to seek attention in other ways or by changes in her family's attitude towards her. She felt taken over by her fears, which turned out to be complexly connected with (for her) intolerable and incessant sexual fantasies. One reason why these fantasies were intolerable was that a split had been created inside her between her 'real self' which was pure, religious and spiritual, and her physical self, which was wicked, demanding and dirty. Her body was not 'her'; her sexuality felt as though it was grafted on to her from somewhere else, and hence was uncontrollable and dangerous, a fire burning inside that could destroy her. All these feelings had correlates with her familial experiences, for example in her repressive and repressed mother, but none of these links was in itself sufficient to explain the the intensity of her fears. Her experiences were 'over-determined', with multiple, complex determinants, mostly outside of consciousness and beyond control. Social and personal themes converged: a family where women were both competitive and unvalued, a girl never developing a sense of herself as separate and strong, a self made false and vulnerable by the intolerable splits on which it was built. To understand complexities of this order more than an appeal to 'attention-seeking' or any other reductive hypothesis is necessary. Only the most personalised yet social of accounts can make sense of an inner world so riven.

Essentialism, then, looks to the individual as the source of meaning and desire without questioning where meanings and desires come from. In Chapter 3 we return to our critique of this position in relation to theories of mental health and 'illness'. Here the task is to develop a non-essentialist account of human development.

THE CONSTRUCTION OF THE INDIVIDUAL

There are several requirements of an adequate theory of individuality. First, it must be developmental, explaining how individuality becomes constructed over time. Second, it must explain consistencies in behaviour, thought and emotion that are demonstrated by all individuals in a society. Third, it must link internal processes and the social forms that give rise to these processes and through which they are expressed. Fourth, it must explain phenomena that surround the apparent breakdown of individuality: divisions of thought and feeling, compulsive and hallucinatory phenomena, creativity and emotional experience. The remainder of this chapter presents a theory fulfilling these conditions, but leaves its application to 'psychopathological' experiences to Chapter 3.

The existence of meanings, thoughts and feelings that do not originate in consciousness (are not 'willed' by the person experiencing them) demands a notion of some causal 'other site' from which internal processes that are not unified in consciousness may arise: a concept of 'the unconscious'. Freud's discovery of the unconscious originated in the recognition of the presence of repressed material – ideas that determine the direction taken by conscious activity, but which are not accessible to consciousness. What distinguishes Freud's psychoanalytic theory is that these ideas are *dynamic*, playing a causal role in thought and behaviour. They are not simply stored away, like books in a library, but are kept from consciousness by continuing pressure (Wollheim, 1971). This is why introspection is never sufficient for explanations of human conduct, even if pursued honestly. Self-observation may be a starting point for enquiry into personal experience, but always runs up against blockages caused by repression. Introspection can generate interesting material, but

> it requires the psychoanalytic dialogue to make sense out of this raw material which is fragmented and unsystematic, and is in its early stages certainly not experienced by either patient or analyst as 'answers' ... Psychoanalysis does not take 'no' for an answer. It aims to make sense of the unknown, perhaps the unknowable.
>
> (Jahoda, 1977, pp. 105–6)

'Making sense' is the enterprise of psychoanalysis. The unconscious is an explanatory concept that gives meaning to phenomena which might otherwise be uninterpretable, such as dreams, symptoms, madness. None of these experiences are under the conscious control of the individual, although sometimes rationalisations may be provided for them after the event, and they are frequently experienced as inexplicable and dangerous, a threat to the integrity of the self. Psychoanalysis gives meaning to these experiences, uncovering purposes or intentions that are unknown to the person experiencing them. Such meanings arise outside consciousness and in that sense are involuntary. This contradicts the common-sense idea of meaning as the product of conscious intention:

> The crux of Freud's discovery is that neurotic symptoms, as well as the dreams and errors of everyday life, do have meaning, and that the meaning of 'meaning' has to be radically revised because they have meaning.
>
> (Brown, 1959, p. 3)

If there is within individuals a system of unconscious materials that are causal and yet outside of conscious control, it ceases to be possible to conceive of humans as unified and whole:

> The unconscious divides and fractures the subject of consciousness. Conduct must always be explained with reference to that *other site* of psychic determination.
>
> (Hirst and Woolley, 1982, p. 133)

According to psychoanalytic theory, at the centre of individuality is a split; behind the boundaries of that split are determining forces, axes around which our everyday actions, emotions and ideas are organised. In general, psychoanalytic approaches move from here to provide the basis for a non-essentialist theory of individuality by regarding these axes as internalised early in development, and hence as social in origin. As Leonard (1984) describes, the usefulness of this developmental scheme is that it reveals how the psyche becomes penetrated by ideological discourses stating, for example, that 'superordinacy and subordinacy' are part of the natural order of things, or that existing class, gender and ethnic relations are right, just and desirable and that alternative arrangements are impossible (Leonard, 1984, pp. 133–5).

There are several psychoanalytic theories of development, some radically opposed to one another. They can be divided into those which stress the conflict between biological instincts and the demands of social reality, those which concentrate on the formation of an 'adaptive ego' with well developed defences, and those which are concerned with the supposed 'primary object-relationship seeking' tendencies of the child, viewing sexual and aggressive impulses as products of this tendency and the social responses elicited by it. For our purposes, some central concepts derived from the first and last of these three positions will be employed, with the details of disagreements omitted in favour of a concentration on usable elements in their general account. It is of interest, nevertheless, to note a dichotomy in recent feminist psychoanalytic writing between those concerned with the 'return to Freud' of the French school headed by Lacan (e.g. Coward and Ellis, 1977; Gallop, 1982) and those working within an object-relations position influenced heavily by Fairbairn, Balint and Guntrip (e.g. Eichenbaum and Orbach, 1982). On the whole, the former group have been theorists, the latter therapists.

All psychoanalytic accounts of development begin from the premise that the child at birth is unable to differentiate her or himself from the outside world, either perceptually or emotionally, and so has to learn through contact with other people and objects where her/his boundaries as an 'I' begin and end. The child is born a chaotic mixture of impulses which are not structured in any particular way, with the exception of some biologically programmed behaviours (sucking, smiling) which themselves wait on experience to acquire meaning. The child is unable to discriminate between internal and external events at first because s/he experiences the self as coterminal with the world in the same way that it was while inside the womb. If the child's demands and desires were always wholly met, this absorption in the universe would remain, for there would be no way of distinguishing an internal state from an external response. However, inescapable circumstances arise which lead a child to feel other than at one with the environment, notably separation and frustration, which create a schism between the child's demands and their gratification. The feelings that these experiences give rise to can seem intolerable to the child – anguish, anxiety and anger. In order to cope, the child employs defences that become basic to the structuring of the personality: repression of desires, or projection of feelings on to the external world. In this way, a discrimination appears between the child's 'self' and the environment, and within the child between what is tolerable and what has to be repressed.

The child's self is therefore structured by a network of defences surrounding her/his experiences with others. As these experiences are themselves socially patterned according to certain underlying but systematic principles (particularly, gender, race and class), the child's self becomes constructed around social axes. In more psychoanalytic terms, the child's 'ego' mediates between desire and social reality in the context of certain specific social relations, with mother and father, for example. In this way, the self is socially constructed. But the notion of construction goes deeper than just our conscious selves. The unconscious also becomes patterned in certain ways through the infant's internalised experiences of relationships with others, whose own defences and responses to the needs and demands of the infant will be governed by their position in the social structures that prevail in particular societies. For example, Chodorow (1978) describes how the structuring of the young female or male child's unconscious desires takes place differently when both are exposed to female mothering in a society structured around gender inequalities. The mother's feelings concerning her femininity, linked as they will be to her own mothering, will be expressed differently with girls and boys, and she will therefore be experienced differently by them. This leads to different patternings of consciousness and defences, the girl, for example, being more likely to become an object of identification for the mother and consequently to have to defend herself against suffocation, the boy being more likely to feel separate and alone. The details of these examples are less important than the general point that the psyche is structured by experiences whose meaning is socially given.

During development, language and symbolic processes are central, creating a being that thinks, acts, feels and recognises itself through the complex pattern of meanings that it has internalised; consciousness ('I') is thus a matter of differentiation, of splitting and channelling in the context of multiplicities of social relations. Psychoanalysts, particularly in the

Kleinian tradition, have provided an extraordinarily rich description of the phantasy world and internal processes of the developing infant. Interested readers might look to Segal (1964) or Bion (1967) for details. However, two points are worth making. First, the psychoanalytic account does not simply describe the development of, as it were, the contents of one's thoughts; it describes the development of thought itself (e.g. Bion, 1962). Thus it does not assume the existence of a pre-given conscious-thinking individual at birth. Second, and relatedly, it sees the infant's thought processes themselves developing out of its relationship to thinking others, particularly the parents. Thus human beings are essentially social in that thinking, speech, symbolic activity are dependent on and in relation to an other – at first an actual other, usually the mother, and later in relation to an internalised other. This explains the accent put on early development and the relative lack of susceptibility to change that adults have: whatever the contents of one's thoughts or feelings, however much these may vary according to age and inclination, if the internalised other(s) one is thinking and feeling in relation to are unchanged, then the basic structure of one's personality will be unaltered and there will be a tendency to revert to repeatedly similar forms of relationships with others ('transference'). Thus the Unconscious is not just what one is not conscious of, but a structure, *socially formed*, that influences and is a precondition of conscious thought and action. Hence Lacan's famous dictum that 'the Unconscious is the discourse of the Other'.

Although Freud's theory of female sexuality has been strongly criticised, psychoanalysis nevertheless provides a clear description of the entry of a social division – gender – into the individual mind, an example of how it can account for systematic similarities between individuals. The meaning attached to sexual difference has powerful effects on how we form relationships and interact with others (and ourselves). Internalisation begins early in life, in the infant's relationship with its parents: 'for the little girl, father is "other", whereas the little boy experiences himself as "other" from the moment of birth because mother relates to him as "other"' (Eichenbaum and Orbach, 1982, p. 23). Such experiences provide the basis for what may appear later to be 'natural' social roles. For example, the identification between mothers and daughters helps create the conditions for women to become 'mothers', with all the connotations that term may have in a patriarchal society.

The most famous of all Freudian concepts, the 'Oedipus complex', can be read as an evocative description of the structuring of sexuality under patriarchy (see Mitchell, 1974). According to Freud, the infant begins life 'polymorphously perverse'; that is, with sexual desires unlocated in any particular valorised body area or directed towards any specific object. This unstructured desire is impossible to maintain in a society that depends on the rational living together of individual humans all with their own desires, so only certain forms of sexual expression and feeling are socially sanctioned. The contradiction between the child's polymorphous perversity and the demands of society materialises in the taboo on incest: in the traditional Freudian account, the male child's desire for his mother is contradicted by the threat of castration emanating from the father, while for the girl child rivalry with the mother for the father's penis is replaced by identification with the mother and the desire for a baby. Whatever the ideological components of this theory, and they are clearly many, the important general point is that the child's sexuality, often assumed to be a 'basic' or essential element, becomes structured over time in relation to others, and hence takes a form intimately connected with social and ideological configurations. Patriarchal relations may therefore be perpetuated despite conscious intentions (Chodorow, 1978) and are implicated not only in social conditioning but in the unconscious relationships present from earliest childhood.

Thus the psychoanalytic account of development includes the notion that society enters into the heart of the formation of the individual. Desire as well as attitudes, unconscious as well as conscious phenomena are organised by social relationships which are in turn structured along certain axes. This theory, then, as well as being developmental, explains consistencies and differences between individuals by linking internal processes and social forms.

The claim that the self is of social origin has both theoretical and political implications:

> if there is no inherent individual to be realized once the shackles of existing social organization are thrown off, then human beings' capacities and welfare becomes a matter of what forms of social organization, what institutions, what practices of training and control can and should exist or be developed.
>
> (Hirst and Woolley, 1982, p. 205)

The abandonment of essentialism means that it is not enough to aim and hope for the revolutionary liberation of human nature: socialist practice must involve the construction of new forms of social relations, and must engage with all levels of human experience.

3
Mental Illness and Mental Health

In this chapter we try to show the relevance of the arguments of Chapter 2 to the development of an adequate theory of psychological 'disorder'. We begin with a critique of some apparently opposed traditional positions which rely on essentialist assumptions, and go on to argue that the psychoanalytic account is of use both in understanding the phenomenology of psychological disorder and in opening up the possibility of a genuinely political understanding of mental health.

MENTAL ILLNESS

The dominant mode of understanding of psychological disturbance, throughout the helping professions, is medical, treating psychological and physical disorder as directly analogous. On this view pathology is identifiable through a set of definable and universally recognisable symptoms that indicate the presence of some underlying disease. Thus a person who shows behavioural characteristics such as 'crying a lot' and 'not sleeping or eating', plus emotional and cognitive states such as 'feeling miserable and hopeless', will be deemed to be suffering from the underlying illness, 'depression'. This is not just a descriptive label, useful because it pulls together a range of factors in a convenient shorthand; rather, the term is explanatory: the presence of symptoms means that the person suffers from an illness that has given rise to them, and which has a potentially identifiable biochemical basis. Although treatment may for pragmatic reasons have to be aimed at the symptoms, the underlying pathology *should be* the target. The symptoms do not have any particular meaning in themselves – no time is spent trying to understand why a woman might have chosen anorexia as one of her symptoms – they derive meaning from the underlying state which they signify. Medically speaking, the anorexia is *because* the woman is depressed, and that's that.

The medical model is shared by organically oriented researchers and medical sociologists concerned to demonstrate the social causes and correlates of mental illness. Even when social 'stressors' are held to give rise to psychological disturbance, the disturbance itself is still usually regarded as an illness (see Brown and Harris, 1978, for a sophisticated account of this kind). Given its hegemony, it is not surprising that there have been a large number of defences of, and attacks on, the medical model of psychological disturbance. Where the defence has not been simply that mental illness is just physical, the tendency is to view the medical approach as a high level integration of all sources of information:

> The medical model, in short, takes into account not merely the symptom, syndrome or disease, but the person who suffers, his personal and social situation, his biological, psychological and social status.
>
> (Clare, 1976, p. 69)

Good psychiatric practice might in fact 'take account' of all these aspects, but such defences are ingenuous on a theoretical level, reducing the medical model to an 'anything that works' pragmatics which belies its ideological basis and which presents it simply as good common-sense. In fact, the medical model has more content than this pragmatism suggests, and its everyday practice is dominated more substantially by its theoretical shortcomings. Furthermore, although we are here primarily concerned with it as an ideological structure, Clare's form of rational defence ignores the substantiality of the medical model at the political level: the necessity in Great Britain of having to go to a general practitioner before it is possible to get psychiatric help, the role of doctors in compulsory admission to mental hospital, and the issuing of sick notes are all examples of political functions of medicine that can only be understood in relation to an analysis of the welfare state. Thus it is important to repeat that criticisms of the medical model are not aimed at individual practitioners, nor are they answerable by the adoption of a more 'reasonable' psychiatric practice. In this sense Clare's liberal defence of psychiatry ignores the materiality of the medical model at both the ideological and political levels.

Criticisms of medical approaches have been numerous, extending from the 'all psychiatry is a plot against freedom' extremism of Thomas Szasz, to more careful historical and conceptual critiques that tease out the normative assumptions of psychiatry and its connection with moral viewpoints of particular kinds (e.g. Foucault, 1967; Sedgwick, 1982). In our view these critiques have persuasively demonstrated the value base of psychiatry and of more general medical models of disorder: that is, it cannot be viewed as an 'objective' science. As has also been pointed out, for instance by Sedgwick, *all* medicine inevitably involves norms and judgements of one form or another which are bound to be related to socially specific norms of health and illness, if only because the 'patients' have to identify themselves as 'ill' in order to take themselves off to a doctor in the first place. Discovery of such norms in psychiatry is therefore not in itself a demonstration of lack of validity as an empirical system. What is crucial, however, is the medical model's connection to the individualistic standpoint criticised in Chapter 2, a standpoint that systematically distorts the understanding of 'mental illness'.

The medical approach has some attractive aspects, particularly its apparent removal of psychological disturbance from a framework of ethical judgement in which people are blamed for their distress or seen as 'bad' rather than 'mad', to the amoral connotations of 'illness'. In theory anyone can be afflicted by a mental illness (although this is restricted in many cases to 'anyone with the right/wrong genes'); it is not their fault and is somehow impersonal, intruding on their lives from outside, something caught in the wind, like a germ. Moreover, having a mental illness entitles the sufferer to medical and nursing care, rather than to punishment. In this respect, the ordinary psychiatric world is far more appealing than the utopias of right-wing libertarians such as Szasz, for whom insanity is a moral choice for which punishment is the appropriate remedy – unless you can pay for your 'problems in living' to be sorted out by a Szaszian analyst. Unfortunately, perhaps because the medical model is built on older and more pervasive mythologies and fears, the elimination of value judgements within psychiatry is lamentably incomplete. For one thing, 'illness' categories such as 'personality disorder' or 'psychopathy' arguably are based on *socially* normative assumptions, the former including odd people who can't be established as ill in any more circumscribed way, and the latter as callous or violent people who show little remorse for their acts and cannot be medically helped. A common defence of psychiatry in the face of this criticism is that diagnoses are on the whole reliable: that is, they can be replicated by other people working under other conditions. However, the simple demonstration that well trained psychiatrists can reach reasonable levels of agreement on the presence of symptoms and on which categories in a classification system to place them in does not bear on whether or not these classifications relate to anything material: it still remains to be established that the categorisation reflects those 'basic' underlying pathologies postulated in medical frameworks. On the whole, this cannot be done: there are remarkably few established, organically describable mental illnesses, despite an enormous research industry throughout the world. Once again, we are not claiming that its non-objective nature makes psychiatry empirically useless; rather, the obscuring of its value base gives it a specious scientificity which represents an attempt to remove it from the realms of social and political analysis.

There is a more pernicious element of social judgement in the medical model that has not received the attention due to it in the critical literature. The medical framework is built on the assumption that symptoms reflect underlying physiological defects which in general have genetic origins, either totally or in the sense that some genetic aberration makes a person vulnerable to mental illness in the face of certain life experiences. Even where genetic origins for disorder are not explicitly theorised, for instance in some 'cognitive' accounts of depression (e.g. Beck, 1976), there is a strong implication that mental illness is permanent and therefore that an individual sufferer is subject to relapses and remissions of their disorder. It is possible that this set of beliefs by itself makes relapse more likely, something that has been proposed as one possible explanation of the better outcome for schizophrenia in non-industrialised societies which do not have such a 'permanent' view of mental illness (World Health Organisation, 1979). In our culture, the place of mental illness as a long-lasting vulnerability is an extraordinarily widespread notion, not just when applied to relatively extreme conditions such as 'schizophrenia', but also to more everyday experiences such as 'nerves'. Rather than adopting a plausible alternative framework, viewing 'nerves' as a response to stress (although this does happen, particularly when people talk about their *own* 'nerves'), related concepts such as 'nervousness' are used alongside character judgements such as being 'highly strung', to suggest that nervous breakdown is not so much a matter of circumstances but of innate constitution. This is one of the most widespread of the connotations of mental illness, and one on which the medical model feeds at the same time as it reinforces it, that the tendency to nervous breakdown, depression, schizophrenia, or whatever, is a permanent tendency, a long-lasting personality trait rather than a passing mishap, an illness more like cancer or diabetes than influenza. The result of these assumptions is that even if there are clear stressors that have 'precipitated' a person's psychological distress, in the end the 'illness' is viewed as residing inside the individual, calling into question all her/his past and future behaviour and position as a rational and reliable human being. For example, consider the impact that a 'nervous breakdown' might have for a teacher's future career, and the attitudes that employers and parents would be likely to develop towards her/him. Or the difference that categorising a woman as a 'depressive' can make to one's analysis of the sources of disorder in her relationship with her husband or of her ability to bring up her children. The politics of these circumstances are obvious: if the final source of discord is within the individual, then it is not a matter for social analysis, nor for consideration of the power relations in which it is embedded. That in most instances characterological ascriptions of permanent states of nervousness or of being 'highly strung' should be applied to women is another statement of the political uses to which these assumptions can be put.

Clearly it would be foolish to pretend that some people do not have a long-lasting tendency to react to stress more extremely than others. However, this does not imply, as the medical model suggests, that they are essentially different from everyone else. The idea that mental illnesses affect individuals who have an unalterable predisposing biological make-up is explicitly essentialist, assuming the origins of disorder to be biological, the environment in which a person develops and lives being reduced to the status of 'precipitant' of 'breakdown'. Psychiatry thus abdicates from the responsibility to make social statements. But there is a more important sense in which naive individualism prevails. As noted earlier, the medical model does not ascribe meaning to the phenomenon of mental illness, other than to see symptoms as signifying an underlying disorder. It concerns itself therefore only with the formal characteristics of symptoms (behaviours, thoughts and emotions) and neglects their content. Thus if a person reports an auditory hallucination, psychiatrists are interested in whether this means that the person is suffering from a recognisable mental illness (schizophrenia); they are not likely to be interested in what the voices are saying, or which parts of the individual's personality they might be representing. This is because psychiatry shares the everyday notion that mental health is characterised by integrity in thought, feeling and behaviour, all governed from some centrally unifying and predominantly conscious 'self', and mental illness by the breakdown of this integrity, of the unified rationality characterising 'normal' human behaviour – 'going off one's rocker' or 'round the bend'. Psychiatry regards disturbances of rationality to be pathological of themselves; its aim is the restoration of a unified consciousness that is in 'control' of psychological functioning. This may seem a worthy aim, but the attempt to achieve it is at the expense of dismissing the content of disturbance as meaningless, and consequently 'treatment' becomes a matter of management or control rather than integration of experience. There is no interest in the subjective experience of mental illness because it is only illness and is as irrelevant to its treatment as the feeling of having a temperature to the treatment of a fever. The experiential component is meaningful only as a clue to the fact that breakdown has occurred and the nature of the disorder. Once that has been established there is nothing left to listen to, for the content of non-rationality is assumed to be non-sense.

Whereas psychoanalysis takes for granted the fragmented nature of the human psyche and prioritises the importance of unconscious material in explaining experience and conduct, psychiatry adheres to the individualism of essentialist theories and can explain irrational phenomena only as aberrations of normal functioning, and thus offers no account of madness or creativity, desire or dream. In contrast to psychoanalysis, which sees psychic integration as a developmental achievement realised unevenly by everyone to greater or lesser degrees in different areas of their functioning, psychiatry takes it as given. This means that whatever the intentions of individual psychiatrists, adherence to a medical model is conformist. Conceptually, the attachment to essentialism and the neglect of unconscious phenomena leave no room for an account of how society enters the formation of the mind, society's role being reduced to stressor or facilitator of human capabilities, with individual differences ultimately restricted to biological ones. Therapeutically, it is conformist partly in its predilection for 'physical' forms of treatment, and partly because it trades in protecting individuals from themselves, increasing the split between conscious and unconscious desires, experience and its meaning. For all these reasons psychiatry must always trade at best in the amelioration of distress; it cannot point the way to change, to a progressively political approach to 'mental illness'.

SOCIAL LABELLING

Radical critics of medical approaches have usually relied on either or both of 'labelling theory' or 'anti-psychiatry' positions. It is not our task to mount a substantial critique of these approaches: this has been done several times by theorists whose political positions are reasonably congruent with our own (e.g. Sedgwick, 1982; Jacoby, 1975). However, we are impressed with the continuing sway that these approaches have in many 'radical mental health' circles: labelling theory continues to be espoused as a plausible alternative to the medical model by many social work trainers and their students, and a substantial number of political radicals still believe Laing to have provided the last word in personal liberation. It may be that this adoption of outworn positions is a reason for the pessimism concerning radical psychology that permeates many of these same circles. In any event, it is clear that these superficially attractive theories do need some consideration here, particularly as many of their defects relate to the same essentialist assumptions that we have criticised when commenting on the medical model.

The virtues and defects of labelling theory are reasonably clear. Labelling theorists have argued that in 'mental illness', as in other forms of deviance, some act is arbitrarily defined by social convention as deviant, the perpetrator of that act is then labelled and defined as an outsider and in turn treats her/himself as such, internalising the labels used by others and acting in accordance with them. An individual might begin by choosing to be socially withdrawn; other people then treat her/him as odd; this image and its resulting experiences (avoidance from others right up to institutionalisation) lead to internalisation of social labels and hence to the beginnings of a schizophrenic 'career'. The power of this approach is its ability to articulate 'secondary deviance', the ways in which social responses exaggerate and mould the initial deviant acts in an interactive manner. Labelling theory thus describes how 'mental illness' is constructed as a set of meanings within specific social environments, and is not some isolatable, molecular 'entity'.

To say that somebody is mentally ill, or to announce oneself as mentally ill, is to attach complex meanings to acts and behaviours.... The accidents of heredity and the blows of

environment do not add up or multiply into the social
position of being 'mentally ill'.

(Sedgwick, 1982, p. 25)

The defects of social labelling theory are also glaring, particularly in the way 'primary deviance' is neglected: what creates
the initial 'odd' act and what determines its social value? In
addition, labelling theories imply that individuals are relatively powerless when faced with social labels, failing to account
for the possibility of different and changeable evaluations of
the same behaviour by different social groups. It also begs the
question of the nature of 'mental illness': supposing organic
syndromes did exist, how else but through observation of
unusual behaviour could they be identified?

An additional criticism is that its account of the 'amplifica-
tion' of deviance assumes that the operation of social messages
is univocal and clear. Social meanings and responses become
internalised through a process of recognition: the individual
notes the responses of the social world to her/his acts,
recognises the 'name' that others give her/him, and applies
that name inwardly to the self. All this is basically conscious
or easily accessible to consciousness; none of it operates at a
deep structural level. It is not therefore simply that the
labelling approach makes the mistake of evaluating individuals as 'judgemental dopes' (Coulter, 1973), unable to
withstand the persuasive power of social labels. It is also that
labelling theory reduces the complexity of relations between
individual and society to simple communications between the
'self' (a unity) and 'society' (a separate unity). The subtle
manner in which social influences construct individuality is
neglected, as are the complications involved in coping with
psychological distress. Labelling theory implies that psychological disturbance may be removed through a renaming of
experience, a change in social outlook or in the individual's
response to the way others see her/him. It cannot account for
the internal experiences of psychological discord, nor can it
comprehend the way in which all forms of social organisation
involve structurings of the psyche that create the conditions
for distress as well as creativity, and which are profoundly

unconscious. In the end, labelling theories are no more than behavioural descriptions of how deviance takes its place in a social network. Essentialist assumptions concerning the unity of individuality and of social attitudes, and neglect of unconscious processes, prevent labelling theorists from giving a psychological account of deviance, nor even an adequate sociological one.

MADNESS AS SANITY

The essentialist idea that human nature requires only the removal of social oppression for it to flower into creative growth has had a powerful hold over theorists more radical than those espousing the social labelling position. There can be little doubt that the supportive psychotherapy that follows logically from the belief that people need only to be provided with a liberating environment has been of considerable help to many indivduals. For example, Carl Rogers's notion that the aim of therapy should be to restore 'congruence' between the split-off parts of the client's personality by providing the conditions of 'unconditional positive regard' which might allow the person to learn to accept her/himself, is quite clearly essentialist and also finally unchallenging – just accept yourself as you are and all will be well. But for people whose experiences of opening out to others have all been of being judged or rejected, the acceptance that goes with this optimistic theory can provide the basis for the first steps to change. The general 'humanistic psychology' or 'growth movement' enterprise, which in part grew out of Rogers's approach to counselling, similarly was and is important in encouraging individuals and groups to look more closely and openly at their personal needs and desires. While the 'psychobabble' excesses of this movement are beginning to provoke an anti-introspection reaction, especially on the macho left, the importance of humanistic approaches for feminists and others should not be minimised. The acceptance of individuals' feelings and the general message that internal needs are significant and that their recognition is an important element in personal liberation and group solidarity, have been crucial stepping stones in linking the personal and the political (see Ernst and Goodison, 1981, for an example of the humanistic technology of feminist self-help therapy). However, it is unfortunate that such views should so often be taken by activists to be the quintessence of political psychotherapy. As the recent spate of feminist psychoanalytic literature has documented, humanistic encounters can only take one so far: once personal blockages are reached that do not respond to simple 'acceptance' by sisters and comrades, then more challenging and correspondingly more *political* approaches become imperative. Personal change is not just a matter of learning to love oneself, although it does help to be convinced that your feelings matter and can be talked about. In fact, total and unconditional acceptance can obscure real conflicts by reducing confrontation to polite conversation – a useful but eventually self-destructive defensive ploy when faced with unpleasant realities. For example, many feminist conscious-ness-raising groups have struggled with issues around jealousy: these cannot be simply wished away or made all right by everyone listening supportively. For change to occur, the roots of this jealousy in social and personal history have to be uncovered, the way in which past experiences are being replicated in the present explored, and the needs and desires that give jealousy its energy identified. All this requires an approach to 'growth' which acknowledges painful facts, and which is willing to confront the unconscious sources of disturbing attitudes and emotions. Humanistic encounters are fine for making people feel better about themselves and their colleagues, but they have little capacity to bring about radical personal and group change (see Illustration 6 in Chapter 4 for an example of some of these issues in practice).

If the practice of 'radical therapy' has often been humanis-tic, its theoretical obeisance has over many years been made to R.D. Laing, who in many circles continues to be regarded as the epitome of anti-psychiatric radicalism (sometimes, ludicrously, being bracketed with Szasz). Laing's theories are considerably more complex and interesting than those of the straightforward growth theorists, but they have similar themes and can be read in similar ways. It is also perhaps no accident that the religiosity present in many humanists (e.g.

Viktor Frankl) is paralleled by the mysticism and escapism of Laing's later works.

Laing's work is best viewed chronologically, as a gradual contextualising of 'schizophrenia' in wider and wider social settings. His first book, *The Divided Self* (1959) begins from the psychoanalytic premise that discourse of all kinds – even 'psychotic' discourse – makes sense if it is listened to, that is, it is intelligible. This is a radical position within psychiatry which, as noted earlier, is committed to a view of psychological disorder as meaningless, the simple breakdown of that rationality which is the only plausible form that 'sense' can take. Laing makes apparently meaningless phenomena intelligible by employing a traditional psychoanalytic framework (the false self/true self distinction used by Winnicot) in conjunction with an existentialist philosophy based on the simple notion that what is crucial for a person is the experience s/he has of her/himself in relationships with others. In Laing's account of insanity, the apparently 'mad' can be understood when placed in the context of the person's experience, in particular those developmental interactions that determine the strength of one's sense of self. There are some remarkable gains made in this book, perhaps the most notable being the undermining of psychiatric assumptions and the clarity with which painful and confusing experiences are interpreted. But there is also a pointer to future problems. Laing's 'method' in *The Divided Self* is exclusively phenomenological; that is, he relies on the accounts given of themselves by his patients. The idea that there may be material that is inaccessible and that provides an even more persuasive context for experience is not considered; in fact, following Sartre, Laing explicitly rejects the Freudian concept of the 'unconscious'. The human psyche is originally whole, becoming split by the interpersonal experiences of the person. It is the clinician's job to heal these splits, to reunify the psyche through therapeutic love. The seeds of later aberrations are already present in this, Laing's most genuinely radical book.

In *The Divided Self*, Laing's radicalism is predominantly psychological, finding meaning in madness by placing it in an inter- and intra-subjective context. His radicalism becomes expressly political when the context used for intelligibility becomes social. Initially, Laing turns to two-person (Laing, 1961) and then family relationships (Laing and Esterson, 1964), exploring the way mystifications in these relationships can give meaning to the schizophrenic experience. Interestingly, as he explores the wider context of the family, Laing's interests become less analytic and less directed towards explanation: *Sanity, Madness and the Family* consists entirely of case histories in which it is supposedly 'obvious' that the schizophrenic child's behaviour makes sense in terms of her experiences, but no attention is paid to why each of the illustrated families have become disturbed. Finally for our purposes, Laing turns in *The Politics of Experience* to the whole mad world as the context for individual insanity. Now 'schizophrenia' no longer exists as a disorder: the world is so destructively, ravingly lunatic that the only sane response is to escape it, either through mysticism or psychotic 'hypersanity'. This book, a favourite of the zonked-out 1960s flower children, is on the surface intensely political (even in the title). Madness is either a conspiracy or a rational response to the perversions of the twentieth century. Laing has here made a leap from insanity as an *intelligible* response, to madness as a *rational* response to circumstances. Madness becomes sanity. This theory does link the most painful of personal experiences with a political account of the world, but the solution proposed is not revolutionary activity in the world, but escape from it into the self, into inner transformation.

Laing's political consciousness apparently extends psychoanalytic thought by bringing to it a commitment to social analysis and change. But it also lacks some of the crucial elements of the psychoanalytic account, and this lack vitiates its power as politics. In particular, whereas Freud traces out in detail the structuring of desire through social relations, Laing relies on a simple opposition between a bad 'society' and a basically good 'individual'. Society is a unitary, out-there (projected) concept: without socially induced distortions the individual would be all-good, the meaningfulness of life would have free expression. In this view the only escape for the individual is through transcendence, the psychotic, psychedelic or mystical 'trip'. Nowhere is there a conception of the individual as split, as other than a good core with the dross of the world heaped on it – an exquisitely humanistic understanding. Nor is there a view of society as complexly structured, through class or gender or in any other way. Society is simply oppressive; it is the maya that distorts our consciousness, which can be escaped when we rediscover the transcendence that comes from within. This mystical rubbish is not just non-radical, it is reactionary: in Laing as in the humanists, political change is reduced to therapy; therapy itself is reduced to consolation.

We have paid extended attention to Laing because his work reflects some of our primary concerns in a distorted way. His theories have all the trappings of political progressiveness: they have pro-human values, they are anti-psychiatric, and they recognise a social context for experiences of distress and personal disorganisation. Yet they end up as mystical and escapist, with Laing himself turning to biologistic speculation and traditional psychiatric practice in the cooler climes of the 1970s (see Sedgwick, 1982). These defects have their sources in Laing's fundamental assumption that inside each of us there exists a unitary, essential self that is not reducible to anything other than what it is, which is good and true, and which is asocial. We view this as humanistic romanticism: there is no inherent, essential individual waiting to be released from social oppression; there are only specific forms of social and personal organisation which intertwine and which provide a complex basis for therapeutic and political struggle.

TOWARDS A POLITICS OF MENTAL HEALTH

Our critique of traditional psychiatric and radical understandings of psychological disturbance has emphasised their reductionism: 'mental illness' is construed in individualistic terms, whether the language used is biological or social. In this section it is argued that psychoanalysis provides a non-essentialist theory of psychological distress and thus fulfils the fourth 'requirement' of a theory of individuality mentioned in Chapter 2 – that of an adequate account of the breakdown of individuality.

An initial deferment to common sense is necessary. There are clearly different levels on which social factors operate, some more obvious than others. There is no doubting the effects of social conditions: considerable evidence attests to the heightened psychological vulnerability of people who are deprived, impoverished or oppressed. Women living in poor conditions with young children and few social supports are several times more likely than better off women to become depressed (Brown and Harris, 1978); children growing up in impoverished inner-city areas are more likely to be disturbed in various ways (Rutter *et al.*, 1975); and women who are unemployed or whose husbands are unemployed have high levels of depression (Cochrane and Stopes-Roe, 1981). Other demonstrable links between social conditions and mental health have been reviewed many times (e.g. Rutter and Madge, 1976) and need not be reiterated here. But it is important to maintain awareness of the overt operation of these social factors, as many adherents of psychoanalytic views have themselves drifted into a different form of reductionism, one which perceives all events as psychologically determined.

Although it is important not to underestimate the effects of social deprivation and overt oppression, there are also more subtle and pervasive ways in which society affects individual experience. Psychoanalytic theory and observation testifies to the continuing power of the unconscious forces around which our personalities are structured during development. Psychological distress and disorder are often the result of early social induction, and unwanted or forgotten ways of thinking or relating can continue to plague us throughout our lives. The psychoanalytic concept of the unconscious, of a radical otherness within the psyche, allows many psychological phenomena to become explicable ranging from the most everyday of experiences (Freud's famous slips of the tongue) through to the most indecipherable insanities. In terms of the politics and therapy that we are concentrating on in this book, there are two major sets of phenomena that are peculiarly important: the breakdown of personality in states of psychological disorder, and the persistent resurgence of ideological values in personal and group relationships.

The most extreme examples of seemingly incomprehensible material are produced in psychosis, for psychiatry epitomised by the rambling incoherences of 'schizophrenia'. Psychoanalysis operates on this material in two ways. The first is analogous to the psychiatric enterprise in that it is concerned with the form of the disorder, although the 'underlying dysfunction' is expressed in psychological rather than biological terms. In this phase of analysis, psychotic symptoms such as hearing voices are interpreted as violent defences employed to ward off an anxiety which might otherwise shatter the individual's precarious self. Internal ideas, impulses or desires are projected on to the world outside so that they need not be experienced for what they are: dynamic forces that undermine the fragile achievement of individuality. For reasons usually traceable to early experiences in which the unpredictability of the world has not allowed a firm discrimination of self–other boundaries, the self has come to be experienced as specious and fragile, at the mercy of hostile or ambivalent desires, which have to be hallucinated as outside the psyche to be controlled. Psychosis is therefore not in itself alien to ordinary psychological functioning (indeed the psychoanalytic theory of groups regards psychotic elements as an omnipresent feature of group functioning); rather it shows the breakdown of defences which enable most people most of their waking lives to distinguish their internal world sufficiently from that which happens outside them to lead ordinary lives while being quietly consumed by desire. Psychosis itself is a 'normal' phenomenon, in the sense of being available to all humans, as the destruction of the self at the hands of untamable and conflicting impulses. In Lacan's (1977) phrase, psychosis is a state in which 'The absence of speech is manifested ... by the stereotypes of a discourse in which the subject, one might say, is spoken rather than speaking' (p. 69).

The second way in which psychoanalysis operates is to examine the expressive elements of psychotic discourse: that is, it enquires as to the meaning of the material that is released by breakdown. In an important way, what the voices say is a significant indicator of the conditions that have given rise to disturbance. Psychotic phenomena are liberated by the breakdown of defences and hence dramatise unconscious desires and conflicts in a manner more powerful and direct than the circumlocutory symptoms of neurosis or of everyday life. By hearing the voices one can gain access to these underground passions and comprehend the personal and social meanings that have culminated in breakdown, but which may not be alien to other individuals whose defences have not been critically weakened. Laing's great achievement in *The Divided Self* was to demonstrate the intelligibility of apparently 'mad' discourse by revealing its interpersonal structures. We follow him in this enterprise, also viewing interpersonal encounters as the source of psychological structures. For example, a pregnant woman who hallucinates that her mother is ordering her to kill her child is telling us more than that she has a fragile ego which cannot cope with powerful emotions. She is also indicating the specific nature of the emotions in question – that they are concerned with destructive feelings. In addition, she is locating their source in the real or fantasised relationship with her own mother, and dramatising the guilty self-hatred which presumably reflects a necessary redirection of hostility away from the mother. There are other possibilities in this scenario, for instance that the woman may be experiencing herself as being taken over by the unborn foetus growing within her and may be linking this with being absorbed into her mother: only intimate knowledge of each case can separate out the relevant interpretations. The main point, however, is a general one, that the expressive elements of symptoms allow access to psychological processes that are meaningful and which supply explanations for personal conduct. These explanations are couched in psychodynamic terms and link the individual's present disturbance with past and present interpersonal experiences. In turn, these experiences are structured in accordance with wider forms of social organisation.

We have picked an extreme example, psychosis, to illustrate points which could nevertheless be made with respect to a wide range of more moderate but distressing phenomena. Although the details of the account would differ in, for instance, the cases of compulsive behaviour or depression, the general principles would remain intact: that unconscious conflicts deriving from early development underlie psychological difficulties, and that the content of these conflicts can be arrived at by exploration of the expressive elements present in symptoms. In this, we go further than traditional psychoanalysis in arguing that particular repressions, organisations of the self and hence pathologies present in any one culture, are produced by that culture, and indicate the specific power relations upon which a society is built and which become inserted into the 'essence' of the individual psyche. Particular forms of social relations produce particular effects, among which is a quantitative impact on the likelihood of distress (highly oppressive societies will produce more despair and psychological breakdown) and a qualitative engendering of particular forms of disturbance. The voices that speak in all forms of psychological disorder provide information not just about the distress of particular individuals, but also about the networks of social relationships along which they resound.

The discussion of individual psychopathology stressed the underlying structuring role of social factors in the development of the individual's 'self'. Apart from an acknowledgement of the important role of current social circumstances in determining the likelihood of breakdown, the role of society in this account is relatively indirect, although crucial. The second issue that we consider here is more overtly social in nature, that of the power of ideological beliefs and strategies to perpetuate themselves over time. This issue has always been of interest to politically radical psychoanalysts. A major motivation for the Freudo-Marxists of the 1930s, notably Wilhelm Reich, was the recognition that despite the apparent occurrence of the 'objective' conditions for revolution in post-First World War Europe, those fermenting societies slipped back relentlessly into authoritarianism and fascism. Probably the major achievement of Reich's chequered career was his analysis in *The Mass Psychology of Fascism* (1975, first published in English in 1946) of the internalised, 'subjective' source of this reaction. According to Reich, authoritarian character structures are developed through experiences in the family, with patriarchal oppression internalised in the formation of the psyche to re-emerge in practice at times of stress.

Reich's argument, that subjective change is essential if objective conditions are to be exploited, is close to our own, even though his conceptual scheme is quite different from ours (we would take issue, for example, with his biologistic emphasis on an undifferentiated sexual instinct, the repression of which is the source of all evil). Time and again, apparently revolutionary situations or parties have revealed the power of traditional relationship structures that have eventually overturned the promise of change. In current political circles the presence within progressive groups of competitiveness and male dominance is only one familiar example of the resistance to change generated by internalised ideological forces; others are present in working-class fascism and in female anti-feminism. Explanations couched solely in terms of current material factors are inadequate for dealing with these phenomena: it is insufficient to designate it as being 'in the interest' of a working-class housewife to be both reactionary and anti-feminist, even though there may be clear ways in which these attitudes reflect her anxieties or unhappiness. One can also not write off the disaffection of many women with the male posturings of the revolutionary movement as due solely to bourgeois preoccupations: their insight that such 'revolutionaries' are themselves replicating the oppressive structures they are so keen to condemn is an essential one for all who wish to bring about change that is genuinely 'radical', that is, to the roots. Earlier we suggested that the failure of many radicals to comprehend the positive functions of power relations which also have negative elements, has contributed to the difficulty in understanding how oppressive structures are maintained. In addition, the traditional Marxist notion of ideology as 'false consciousness' has limited understanding of the power of belief systems that appear self-destructive to be perpetuated. 'False consciousness' suggests that some effort of will, or at least of correct education, will be sufficient to cast off ideology and see the 'truth' – which is that society is dominated by economic relations of specific kinds. Correspondingly, as ideology is superstructural, economic changes will automatically bring about changes in belief systems; the transition to socialism will enable us to cast off false consciousness in favour of scientific, materialist objectivity. Unfortunately, it seems more likely that without changes in ideology, no such transition to socialism will ever take place.

As argued in Chapter 1, ideology is not simply a set of inaccurate perceptions. Moreover, although it is important not to reduce the unconscious to an internalisation of ideology, we follow Althusser in his argument that

> In truth, ideology has very little to do with 'consciousness', even supposing this term to have an unambiguous meaning. It is profoundly *unconscious* ... Ideology is indeed a system of representations ... but it is above all as 'structures' that they impose on the vast majority of men, not via their 'consciousness'. They are perceived-accepted-suffered cultural objects and they act functionally on men via a process that escapes them.
>
> (Althusser, 1965, p. 233)

Ideology is structural, yet it operates internally on people through 'a process that escapes them'. Our account of a psychoanalytic view of unconscious structuring allows this process to be understood: through the experience of being 'dipped into' a social flux structured by certain power relations and ideological practices, the individual psyche becomes organised along lines consistent with these structures. Early projections and introjections, later Oedipal conflicts and their resolution, channel the infant's desires into socially permitted realms, at a level of personality not immediately accessible to consciousness. Certain ideologies dominate because during development they become the axes around which personality is structured, the discourses through which desire is produced, and not just through social conditioning or identification with parental attitudes or cultural images. This developmental construction of the individual helps insert her/him into the dominant ideological practices and power relations of society, and accounts for much of the latter's resilience. An example will illustrate why this is so.

As described in Chapter 2, under patriarchy the infant boy's experience of himself as 'other' and the infant girl's experience of herself as 'same' in relation to a mother who has herself internalised existing patterns of ideology provides the basis for a set of relations built around the recognition of gender. Let us suppose that the experience of separateness leads the boy to feel that he has to control his emotions because there is no one to share them with. This in turn is likely to lead to a fear of losing control, particularly when alone, which may be compensated for or defended against by a fantasy of being with, getting inside and controlling an idealised mother from whom he is not separate but part of. The absence of such a figure in real life may then lead to a search for her in relationships where the man repeatedly both idealises and attempts to control women. This repetition, even if noticed by the man or others around him will not be accessible to conscious changes of attitude towards women unless the unconscious basis for it (fear of separation and its associated repressed fears, fantasies and emotions) is some-how addressed. This man's psychic structure, however, neatly inserts him into a multitude of discourses, practices and power relations that produce men as dominant and in control, women as submissive and 'emotional'. It is this 'match' between the man's psychological make-up and the social relations he becomes subject to that accounts for the constant reproduction of the latter, even when the overt external forces maintaining them have been removed. Thus suppose we take pornography as an example of a discourse that typically portrays women as passive objects of male control. The man may consciously reject pornography on moral or political grounds and yet still find it exciting, or that he manifests his unconscious attitudes towards women in other aspects of his behaviour, e.g. in conversation, jokes, etc. Furthermore, any attempt to attack these attitudes is likely to arouse the unconscious anxieties against which his image of women is a defence and therefore likely to create strong resistance. This is not to say that there is no point in political campaigns against pornography, which as a discourse is maintained by all sorts of factors that have little or nothing to do with the upbringing of men; it is, however, to emphasise the way internal and external forces combine to prevent change.

The example just given, irrespective of the accuracy of its rather simplistic developmental theorising, illustrates not only the recalcitrance of power relations but also the relationship between the psychoanalytic theory defended in this and the previous chapter and the analysis of power and ideological practice of Chapter 1. It can be seen that the psychoanalytic unconscious is not just a product of ideological practice, but that in any specific instance analysis must be made of both and the ways they intertwine. Thus, in our example, the man's increased political awareness did not necessarily produce an increase in self-awareness, and an understanding of this requires both political and psychoanalytic concepts.

It is because on the one hand the unconscious is more than an effect of ideology, and on the other that ideology is more than a manifestation of human psychology that it is incorrect to reduce the social world to the psychological or vice versa. Moreover, it is only in so far as it is possible to conceive of the two realms as interrelated but not equivalent that it is possible to conceive of a change in that relationship; if the two were no more than reflections of each other the outlook would indeed be gloomy, for change can only take place through contradiction. Although we have emphasised the complexities of bringing about change, our view is optimistic in its suggestion that political activity can legitimately be directed towards internal as well as external power structures. We are therefore in accord with feminists who argue that power relations between and within individuals are as important a political target as power relations with the state. Alteration of personal relations, it is true, will never be sufficient for radical political change because the state plays a major role in organising and controlling them; but changing large-scale power structures is also insufficient on its own because of the social structuring of subjectivity revealed by psychoanalysis and reproduced at all levels of social intercourse.

Psychological disorder, then, must be seen in the light of processes of social induction undergone during development and reinforced in ideological practice; individual suffering may represent universal experiences of power and oppression. Therapeutic and political practice are thus knotted together and must attempt subversion in a double sense: not just of here-and-now social reality, but subversion of the past as lived out in the here-and-now. The following chapters examine the problems this poses for the development of a radical mental health practice.

4
Therapy, Personal Change and Struggle

Our concern in this and the following chapter is to formulate ideas on the nature and implications of a politically conscious mental health practice. We have argued that personal and political change are intertwined, although neither is reducible to the other, and that therapy can be linked to politics through its exploration of the roots of action and emotion. In practice, however, it often privatises experience, hiding individual unhappiness without challenging the social structures that have given rise to it, and without encouraging links between individuals sharing the same distress. While this is an easy criticism to make, it is less obvious what the alternatives are, and it is with the aim of exploring this question that this chapter analyses examples drawn from our work in terms of both their psychological and political significance. The themes that emerge are further developed in Chapter 5.

THE ILLUSTRATIONS

The illustrations that follow are descriptions of work carried out by the authors. The first three are accounts of therapeutic interventions in conventional psychiatric, social work and community health settings. Collectively, this group is entitled 'Therapy and personal change' to emphasise the individual focus of the work in each case. The second group of three examples, entitled 'Therapy and struggle', describes interventions and experiences with more explicitly political content and consequences, despite their emphasis on psychological change. The illustrations were subjected to a process akin to the psychoanalytic interrogation of emotions, defences and attitudes. As a group the pieces were examined for therapeutic and political implications, for the assumptions the author brought to the work and writing, the resistances and conflicts displayed, and the discourses that helped construct the apparently 'personal' experience described. The more each piece was examined, the less homogeneous it appeared, words and turns of phrase taking on increasingly complex significance. This produced a mass of material, not all of which can be reproduced here. However, summaries of the analyses are given at the end of each illustration, with an overview after each sub-section. The pieces have deliberately been left in their original, uneven, uncorrected form. All names and identifying details have been changed.

THERAPY AND PERSONAL CHANGE

Illustration 1: Individual psychotherapy: Mr A

Mr A is a thirty-five-year-old Irishman whom I have been seeing for individual psychotherapy for approximately five months. The summary I give below is obviously selective and presents an oversimplified view of the progress of therapy, which has been far more muddled and difficult than would appear. My summary is also only my view of what has gone on, what has been significant, and Mr A would probably have a very different story to tell. The validity of one's interpretations of events can only be demonstrated by what happens next, not by a retrospective account such as this, which inevitably sees much that has gone before in terms of what now seems to be the situation.

Mr A had been on antidepressants for some months before being referred to me, and although he was now back at work, as a commercial banker, he had been off work for several months earlier in the year, suffering from 'depression'. His appearance was neat, he wore a suit that was neither too casual nor ostentatiously smart. He tended to speak in a rather abrupt, impatient way, but he also seemed desperate not to offend me, lest perhaps I should tell him to go away. He came from a strict Catholic family, with a stern, intolerant, sometimes violent father who dominated the household and whose main concern was to get them out of the poverty in which they were living (which he managed to do). Mum was an undemonstrative, mysterious figure who, though she seemed to love her children, found it hard to express and never let show any emotions or personal details of her life: 'She didn't cry when Granny died', Mr A said, confused and angry. There were four younger sisters and a younger brother, but so far they haven't figured much in the therapy.

Mr A had completed a questionnaire about his difficulties and background before seeing me, and what was most striking about it was on the one hand that his description of his own problems was curiously metaphorical (his depression began with an incident on holiday with three other men where they had been able to ride bicycles and he hadn't, and he'd consequently felt left out), but on the other his description of his life and family was completely in terms of facts: no information about his character, the characters of his family or his feelings about any of them were included, just facts and figures.

Mr A had moved down to London, hoping for promotion, some years back, but had found it hard to settle here, and it soon became clear that he would have a better chance of promotion if he returned to Ireland, which he had just applied to do when he started seeing me. This was to be the answer to his problems. He accepted my suggestion that he came weekly for a fixed period (twelve appointments) at which time we would review the situation in the light of whether he was to be returning to Ireland, and of how therapy was progressing. He expressed surprise that I thought therapy might take as long as three months, so much so that he took my suggestion of twelve appointments as a promise that he would be better after that time, and wanted to know why it would take so long, how he'd know when therapy was completed, etc. As he later said himself, at this time his conception of therapy was of some *thing* that would be done to him, or given to him, to make him feel better. Naturally, he was anxious about what to talk about when he came, wanted to know how it would help him to talk about his problems; I had simply said to him to try and talk about whatever was on his mind. Despite his protests at my not answering his questions directly but interpreting them on the one hand as being due to a fear of doing things wrong and perhaps being punished by me, being left abandoned and no better, and on the other hand as being a desire on his part to have control and certainty of the progress of therapy before it had even started, Mr A attended regularly and promptly. A pattern of sorts established itself: for a week or two he would complain that I wasn't helping him, that I didn't understand, that seeing me just made him feel worse, that he'd been in despair throughout the week, that I was criticising him. Then would come a week when he would arrive beaming and announce that he thought therapy was at an end now because he felt fine, so much so that there was nothing he had to say today, and he thought he'd better not waste my time by continuing to see me. His changes in mood were sometimes attributed to me rather unconvincingly, and in fact were experienced by him as arbitrary and uncontrollable – so much so that he was astonished when I pointed out to him one week the discrepancy between last week's total despair and this week's euphoric optimism.

The major incident in his life that occurred in the first couple of months was his interview concerning his application to be transferred back to Ireland. He expected automatic promotion and was furious and very upset by this seeming to be out of the question until he had undergone a probationary period at his new post. He felt let down, undervalued, not without justification. He also felt personally got at in a way which seemed in excess of the facts. Although a slightly harsh decision, and one which may have been altered if he had been given wholehearted support from his manager, who apparently didn't want to risk offending Head Office by protesting at the decision, as presented it didn't seem wholly unreasonable and didn't seem to warrant the extreme rage and despair it provoked. He became quite wary of any contact with other people, and any comment I made was taken as lacking understanding and critical. His state of mind was well expressed by an anecdote he told me of how, when he'd been depressed earlier in the year, it was funny but when he walked to work he took the subway to cross the road even though it was a longer walk than taking the pedestrian crossing – but, after all, with pedestrian crossings you could never tell whether a car would stop for you or run you over. He experienced people as unpredictably hostile and dangerous, about to run him over at any minute, even if he was acting reasonably, and so he 'went underground', presented the appearance of a mild, quiet, inoffensive character who generally avoided contact with others, and would never exchange a cross word with anyone. To himself he pretended that he needed no one, and although he would accuse me of making him feel worse, or of having no effect on him whatsoever, he never acknowledged any desire or need to come, except that he hoped it would somehow 'cure' him in the end.

A recurrent feature of the sessions was that right towards the end, an apparently vital burning issue would arise, and despite my saying, 'We have to stop now' to indicate that the session was over, Mr A would carry on talking for a minute or two before leaving. Alternatively, as he was putting on his coat to leave he would try to engage me in a friendly conversation – about the health service strike, or the weather, or my holidays – and this would continue for a minute or two before he left. At first I permitted this, though feeling rather uncomfortable as to what was going on: no doubt there were burning issues left undiscussed, no doubt he did feel friendly, but I felt confused as to what was going on, and awaited the opportunity to broach the subject in a way that he wouldn't experience as persecutory. Two sessions followed before I did so. In the first he criticised me for sitting there saying nothing, resulting in long silences; I responded that he seemed to take my silence as a criticism, rather than as my allowing him the space to use as he wished. The second session was characterised by long silences as if he was deliberately trying out a new strategy.

In the next session Mr A began talking again about how depressed he'd been by not being offered promotion, and how unsympathetic I had been towards him. I replied that although he talked about it as a naturally upsetting event, that was a great blow to his self-confidence, and although I wasn't denying that this was to some extent the case, I thought that it was more than that, that what his job represented to him was the possibility of his having absolute control over his feelings, situation and other people, and that he felt thwarted in this ambition for power, which if realised would mean that he could feel all right without the need for other people. I said that I thought what he wanted was not just due recognition of his abilities, but to be the top person, in control of everything, and that he did the same in therapy when he continued the sessions past their time; it was as if he was saying, 'I'll determine when the session ends, not you', and that by doing this he could go away feeling he had triumphed over me, been in control after all. Visibly taken aback, he said that when he went to work he resented having to arrive and leave at a specified time. At the end of the session he left promptly, stopping only to nod a friendly goodbye.

The next session began with a long silence, which was broken by him saying that he'd been thinking about what I'd said last week about his wanting power over other people, and that he thought I was probably right. I replied that I wasn't sure whether that was such a difficult thing for him to say as he'd made it seem, but perhaps what he was feeling more was a slightly schoolboyish feeling of having been found out – to which he burst out laughing and said yes, that was exactly what he was feeling. He began to talk about his fear of losing control, and when asked what his worst fantasy was of what would happen he said it was like clearing up the office, that if he left others to do it without his being in charge then they might do it all wrong and the inspectors might be brought in to clamp down on what was going on. I asked him whether he was saying that if he relinquished control over the mess in him that needed clearing up, then other disturbing parts of himself would do it all wrong, attack him rather then help him, and that these were only manageable by 'bringing in the inspectors' to punish him; that he seemed to have no faith that there might be something good in him that might help manage things; and that the only way he could feel all right about things was to lay down the law severely in the way that his father seemed to have done, rather than through some more caring, understanding attitude such as he had sometimes described his mother as having provided. There felt like a very moving contact between us, and he began to talk about his mother for the first time, not in idealised terms but about how he couldn't understand her, how he supposed she did care but it was very hard for him to experience it. Again, the session ended on time, as have all the following ones.

The next week he came in saying that nothing had happened of any significance in the past week, that he felt fine, things had been going well at the office, he hadn't felt got at, that he was applying for other jobs in London, and was beginning to realise that he would lose a lot by leaving London. Although he still thought he would go to Ireland if he couldn't find a better job in London, he thought that his desire to move to Ireland had been partly an attempt to run away from his problems, that he acted as if everything bad was to do with London and everything would be all right if he went back home. The past two weeks had indeed seen a remarkable change in his demeanour: he was far more relaxed and cheerful than I had ever seen him. He said he didn't know why he was feeling so different but he hoped it would last, and that he felt superstitious about discussing anything with me in case it made him feel worse, although he didn't really think it would. After four months getting at me for not saying anything he was suddenly telling me not to speak! I said to him that it seemed the way he'd felt the past two weeks was quite different to how he'd felt, certainly throughout the period of seeing me, and from his description different to how he'd felt for a year before that. He agreed, and I said that he found it hard to acknowledge either that the therapy may have had some effect on him or that he had any potentiality in himself for coping – it was all luck. I also pointed out that despite feeling so different to how he'd felt for years, which if true seemed to me an event of potentially great significance, what he actually did was to come to the session and say that nothing had happened. After a pause he replied that one of the good things about the past week was that he hadn't felt absolutely desperate to come to see me, which he had for the first few months (a rather backhanded acknowledgement of dependence!). Now he thought that perhaps the reason he was feeling different was because of coming to see me. In particular, he'd been thinking a lot about what I'd said about his wanting power over other people, and that it was something he'd never admitted to himself before, but admitting it seemed to have made him feel different. He still wasn't sure what had made him feel so different, though, it seemed so intangible, and he agreed with me when I recalled how when he first came he was so eager to get something tangible to make him feel better – a prescription, advice, promotion. He said he now thought it wasn't that simple, that he'd started to think differently about things. I said that I thought he was still understandably anxious that he might suddenly feel awful again and that there was some sense of his wanting to relax and enjoy how he felt at the moment, to mark time for a while and not risk rocking the boat while he was here, so he was hoping that I wouldn't say anything that would upset him. The session ended.

Comments on 'Individual psychotherapy'

The major issues in this account are those of therapy as 'magic', the uses of power, and the extent to which the feelings of the therapist are caught up in the events of therapy. Therapist and client appear to agree that therapy is something special, a process outside of them with its own logic, acting in a manner which cannot be disclosed except in an 'oversimplified' way. Such is clearly the case for the client: his conception of therapy was 'of some *thing* that would be done to him, or given to him, to make him feel better'. The client had taken on board the notion of his unhappiness as an illness, and to some extent this provided relief by suggesting that there might be something tangible and immediate that could be done about it. On the other hand, the illness metaphor is alienating in that it splits off parts of the client's personality from his control, accentuating the experience of therapy as a kind of 'operation'. But the therapist also colludes in the mystification of therapy. The phrase 'individual psychotherapy' at the start of the illustration raises a set of assumptions and sets the context for something special and complex. This is supported by the word 'oversimplified', which nevertheless fails to specify what that complexity might be. The phrase 'how therapy was progressing' is the therapist's phrase, not the client's, making therapy sound as if it is something

concrete outside the relationship between the two protagonists, having its own course. This fits in with the client's idea
that therapy is something that will be done to him. What is at
issue here is not just that the therapeutic process is not fully
described, but that by setting therapy up as something
esoteric, by mystifying its processes and failing to explain the
rationale behind specific interventions, the striking change
brought about apparently by one interpretation takes on a
magical quality. It is located in no clear interactive context,
has no established mechanism of operation, but suddenly
reorganises the client's consciousness. The danger in this is
that the alienating aspect of therapy becomes dominant, and
it appears as another 'magic bullet' approach.

Much of the therapeutic interaction that is presented in the
illustration centres on issues of power. On the surface this is
concerned with relations between the client and the outside
world, in particular the way in which he feels oppressed by his
work environment and endangered by the hostility and unpredictability of people he might encounter. But there are two
important ways in which power surfaces within the therapeutic situation as a major issue, one recognised and one possibly
not. The first of these concerns the battle between therapist
and client for control of the session: the therapist, with his 'my
summary is only my view' pretends to tolerate dissent, but
actually experiences discomfort over his inability to control
the client. Eventually he interprets the client's behaviour in
the session as a bid for control. This interpretation is clearly a
turning-point, receiving immediate confirmation in the behaviour of the client and liberating him to express his feelings
differently. But it is also unusually aggressive. The therapist is
accused of being 'unsympathetic', a stance that is in some
ways justifiable in terms of the gains that are derived from the
'unsympathetic' interpretation: it isn't enough just to be nice
to people. But the interpretation is more than just unsympathetic: it bursts out of the therapist, triumphant and
energetic, persecuting in content if presumably not in delivery, a turning of the power tables to put the therapist back in
control. The absence of any substantial comment on the
therapist's feelings in this account makes it impossible to
judge the extent to which the interpretation had subjective,

unrecognised origins in the therapist himself; at least, it is conceivable that some of the energy of the interpretation derives from the therapist's concern that his power is being threatened.

A second sense in which power issues are played out in the session is in fact closely related to the first, as it refers to the boundaries placed on the session by the therapist and the kind of material that is seen as legitimate. Despite the client's concern with work, the therapist early on tells us about his family, making the psychotherapeutic assumption that family background is crucial, that knowing the family scenario, from however long ago, allows one to 'place' the adult more thoroughly than, for example, knowledge of their work or political affiliations. Later on, the client's new ability to talk about his mother is taken by the therapist as an indication of the progress that has been made, although the client's definition of the significant issues may well not have changed. The therapist is permitted to refuse to answer questions, although if the client behaved in this way his refusal would receive an interpretation. The therapist presents his own refusal simply as a technique, with his feelings at being put under considerable pressure by the client's questioning being edited out of the account, and the interpretation provided to the client actually misses out the positive elements of the client's challenge to the therapist by emphasising the therapist's knowingness and control rather than his defensiveness. Finally, it is in the therapist's power to determine the reality of the client's feelings: he is 'unconvinced' by the client's attributions of the sources of his change of mood; he knows what silences mean; he can establish when things that are said should be taken as having meanings other than their surface ones. It is obviously an important element in a therapist's technique simply to make accurate judgements about which feelings are genuine, and to understand the various ways in which a client might be trying to express something. In this illustration, however, the fact that such judgements are being made is left unacknowledged, thus obscuring the sense in which what is going on involves the exercise of power by the therapist over the client.

The final point to be raised here has already been alluded to in various examples above. A major reason why so much that goes on in the illustration is mysterious is that it is not properly contextualised in the relationship between therapist and client. Obviously, the major interpretation concerns this relationship, but it is written up in a curiously one-sided way. Perhaps because of feelings of having to justify his activity, or assumptions about professional impartiality or objectivity, the therapist has omitted to give sufficient space to his own input into the relationship with the client. As the example of the major interpretation reveals, it is probably not the case that the therapist's behaviour is governed solely by responses to the client's actions; he also brings something of his own to the encounter. Much of a therapist's skill presumably lies in being able to separate out those feelings that are genuinely engendered by the particular individual with whom s/he is confronted, and those that are part of the therapist's personality. By editing out his feelings from the text, the therapist in this illustration provides no evidence on which a judgement of his rationale for interpretation can be made. Without the relational context, the text can be construed as power games; with it, it might have a logic of exploration and de-alienation through the way in which one person is touched by, contains and regenerates another.

Illustration 2: Therapy in social work: Carol

Carol is the mother. She is of medium height and slim build, with a give-away bulging stomach, which is evidence of loose muscles from the children she has born, rather than of overeating. The rest of her body is scrawny. Her dress and make-up are crude to the point of caricature: bright, greasy lipstick that smells of cheapness and oversteps the line of her actual lips; eyelids covered in gashes of bright blue powder with bits of glitter which have always fallen carelessly over her cheeks and onto her nose. Her hair is very thin and stuck up with grease, it is dyed and her scalp shows through. Her uneven, mottled skin is outrageously covered in dark brown make-up, which leaves streaks of her deathly pale colour underneath. The garish effect of this pathetic attempt at beauty mainly outlines the rottenness of her teeth; they are a nutty brown colour and caked with the gunge of food and decay which indicates that they are simply never brushed. Her clothes reflect the same style of 'fashion' through the hopelessness of jumble sales. Carol frequently has bare legs in the middle of winter and wears huge platform-heeled plastic shoes which rub large pussy sores into her feet. Her finger nails are bitten away, and her arms and hands are constantly covered in deep cuts and scars – she has endless accidents which give her something to go to casualty about, and something to be proud of. Carol tells me that she has weekly wins at bingo, she smokes a lot and will not live long past forty. She takes no care of herself, and her health is very poor. Carol is thirty-five.

Carol's family have always been of concern first to the child-care department, and over the last twelve years to the Social Services. She has produced many babies, as did her mother, and cannot care for them either physically or emotionally, being little past the infant stage of development herself. The years matured Carol a little, and in her late twenties she started living with a man who fathered two more of her children. He was a kind man, very limited in his expectations and understanding of the world, but nevertheless aware of the need for regular food and warmth. His presence and the support of nurseries and school allowed Carol to care for these two children. However, when they reached the ages of five and six, he left. The care they had received previously was barely adequate, but subsequently they were frequently unfed and never washed. They became scapegoated at school for smelling, and often were found on the streets playing or knocking on doors asking for food from neighbours. Several referrals were made to the NSPCC, and the flat was found to literally resemble a rubbish tip, with old food, newspapers, rags and cat excrement jumbled up in a hideous chaos. The sheets on the children's beds were always soaked in urine, and there was no sign of food being bought or prepared there. It seemed that Carol and her two daughters were in the relationship of three competing small children, each with enormous needs of nurturance, care and love; each hungry but with little to give except the most impulsive offering, which receded as quickly as it came. Carol as the mother was, of course, expected to care for the other two children – she was no more equipped to do it than they. Nurturance had never been given to her as a child, and therefore she was at the stage of making impulsive demands, as she felt them, for love, comfort, food; the only difference seemed to be that for her this now included sex. It is often said that three is a difficult number – one will be pushed out, excluded – the weakest, the one endowed with the least attributes for power and success. The eldest child was this very person; she was plump and clumsy, fair and blue-eyed like her sister and mother, but unattractive – her features were rough and uneven and she wore thick glasses due to very bad eyesight and a squint. At the age of seven she was talking about killing herself, and her phantasies contained gory and violent images. I have no doubt that these were communicated between mother and daughter and encouraged, but mother had learnt to conceal them, thereby maintaining a very slim veneer of 'normality'. These manifestations of disturbance in a child of seven were intolerable to those around her, and the girls were removed from home and immediately placed with a short-term foster family. Carol was angry but did not seem to mourn them; she did not engage legal help and her defence was non-existent: simply, she was their mother.

The children underwent a shockingly speedy transformation; they became clean, round and polite, chatty but controlled. They needed no help to decipher the new rules whereby they would gain approval, they launched themselves wholeheartedly into fitting in. It was a question of survival. Shortly after the start of this placement I started a series of ten weekly sessions with the children, with the aim of helping them make more sense of their past: the anger, the guilt, the fear; allowing its expression and thereby moving on to a new future.

I arrived at the beginning of each session with a roll of huge paper, a bundle of thick, brightly coloured felt tips, glue, scissors, several 'families' of flexible felt dolls, orange juice and biscuits. They knew immediately that the time was for them, and without fail used the hour to forgo their new-found behaviour and act out the feelings that were just below the surface.

Each session they would come into the room feeling tight; Ann, the younger, would often be angry and sullen, Yvonne usually sad. Within minutes of welcoming them in, establishing what lesson they were missing and that they minded being different from the other children, they would quickly remove their shoes and don the roles of 'Supergirl' and 'Superbaby'. For several minutes this entailed clambering on all the furniture, racing round, holding hands and laughing. They initiated and seemed to need this warm-up period. The game would then become more sinister. They would both approach me menacingly and after initially receiving some very hefty blows, I had to establish a no-hitting rule. 'Pretend hitting' would have to be used in its place, although throughout the time I frequently had to remind them of this, their need to lash out was so strong.

They would then 'overpower' me and either 'tie' me up or cast a spell on me using their superpowers which would immobilise me completely. They would then proceed with accompanying detailed description to cut off my hands and feet and generally disembowel me; each session contained different variations on the same theme. The experience was obviously thrilling to them, they became excited and emotionally high, charged with a glorious feeling that they had eventually been offered a space in which to experience their own sense of power. At this stage they could only use it sadistically and in a very uncontrolled way. After about a third of the session had been used in this way, I would start to renegotiate the balance of power. I would assert, for example, that their spell was slowly losing its effect, or that I had my own magic to repair the damage done to my body. They always found it hard to accept and always feared that I would annihilate them with my power as an adult, as I had destroyed their family by removing them from their mother. I always felt it was important to win their agreement and found that the felt tips were useful in this respect. In the first sessions they were my 'magic sticks' which I willingly shared with them as an enticement to move on to another stage; but they quickly learnt that if they grabbed the sticks before I did, that

I wouldn't grab them back, but that they could give me some, albeit fairly reluctantly. In this way I thought they learnt to share a little, and could experience that even when I had as many sticks as them, I still respected them as people. Not only that, when I had regained my power in the session they could feel safe enough to continue to explore these frightening feelings.

The next stage of each session was calmer and quieter and more frightening for the children. In spite of my reminder at the beginning of the session to use the toilet, they both felt a need to escape for a few minutes at this point. I suggested to them that they didn't necessarily need the toilet but needed a break from what we were doing, because they felt frightened. They never denied this.

On their return I would initiate a game, in the earlier sessions it was usually the telling of a story. I would set the scene and the characters, usually a Mummy and her two children (maybe bears or cats or even creatures from a different planet), and then I would pass the telling on to one of them. In this way we would go round and round, taking turns until they felt the story was completed. Usually the mother died and the two children were whisked away by a fairy godmother, to a beautiful house with lots of beautiful things. At this stage I felt that their feelings and imaginations were informed by the kinds of stories that they had heard. However, they eventually told a story in which the mother was attacked by a horrible plague and died a very painful death, the two children were turned into angels and floated up to paradise where there were lots of beautiful things to eat and play with. Everyone there was happy. However, instead of dwelling on aspects of this idyll, the two children looked down to where they had come from, and could see a deep blackness, filled with writhing snakes and evil forms, erupting volcanoes and enormous turbulence. The vividness with which they described this painful hell was striking. This seemed to mark a turning point in the sessions, and they were subsequently more ready to look forward to their fantasies about a new family, as well as express a lot of guilt about having left their mother, and fear about how she was coping without them.

At times one or both of the children would be unable to

partake in any of these activities, obviously stuck with a feeling which felt too frightening to come out. On these occasions I would draw a picture of the two children with big bubbles (cartoon-style) coming out of their mouths. This enabled them once-removed to express the anger and sadness that they felt. It was a process by which they gained much relief and could still be used with them to great effect a year after they had been placed with a permanent foster family.

Towards the end of the ten weeks, the girls had a less acute need to be so vehemently destructive of me, and also found the process of relinquishing their autocracy a little easier. They began to feel freer to manipulate the dolls, initially joining all of them into a ball of humanity and then aggressively destroying the security they had created. Later on they set them up as characters, being cruel as well as loving to each other.

By the eighth session it was established that the children were to move to a new family on a long-term basis, and again their use of the sessions changed. They were frightened and excited; they felt chosen and lucky, but there was also a marked increase in their guilt about their mother. At this point I brought two large scrapbooks to the sessions, and with photographs, stories and drawings we began to account for their history from babyhood.

Lastly, and in passing, at the end of each session, myself and the two girls would clear everything away and have orange and biscuits. This was comforting to them. It was a gift from me for all the work they were doing and it had an easing effect for them, which helped them re-enter the world of school, from which they had taken an hour's respite.

Comments on 'Therapy in social work'

This illustration has a vivid and distinct pictorial quality which makes it the most energetic of all the pieces presented in this chapter. But it is also from this same intensity that some of the problematic themes arise. The very vividness of the piece obscures some of the processes and consequently makes scrutiny difficult. For example, how is the ideology of the agency reproduced by the worker? To present an illustration of work without clearly identifying the agency involved is to perpetuate the view that professional work takes place in a void, uncluttered by the objectives and ideology of the agency to whom the worker is accountable. Clearly, a central dynamic of any form of interaction is the interaction between the client, the worker and the agency. How, for example, can we explain the way in which Carol is presented? Carol is from the start presented as an object: 'Carol is the mother'. In trying to convey the real Carol she in effect becomes a caricature. 'The garish effect' does convey a lot; it highlights not only a sense of shock that Carol exists, but also an attempt to distance the worker's feelings from those of the client. The reduction of Carol to an object is not simply a function of the worker's complicated feelings towards her, but it also reflects the views of the state towards Carol. First, as a mother her role is to reproduce in her children society's dominant values – an object in the process of social reproduction. The state's role is in effect to manage this process. When Carol fails, for whatever reason, her role is taken over by the state, and she is to all intents and purposes criminalised, medicalised and forgotten. She is redundant. The worker's rationale for working with the children is rooted in her annihilation of Carol as a worthwhile person. Even the description of Carol 'being little past the infant stage' is not sufficient for her to get the help and attention that is offered to her children. Furthermore, 'being little past the infant stage' may sound plausible enough but disguises the fact that a judgement is being made about what maturity is: implicitly Carol is condemned by state and worker alike.

The stage is set for the worker to substitute, albeit symbolically, herself for the mother (and the state), as she is intent on rescuing the children and protecting their future. The past and Carol become distorted by the process of therapeutic exchange (play) and are simply expressed via fantasy. This is not to suggest that the use of play and fantasy are not useful therapeutically, but rather to point out how Carol and her life and experience cease to exist materially for the children. Clearly, when children are removed from parents, the worker very often has considerable difficulty in working with the parent/s. The point to make here, and it is not made in the illustration, is that the worker, under the guise of therapeutic intervention, renders Carol absent, while, in the process, Carol becomes for the children a source of guilt.

The writer's feelings about the children and her acute perception of their distress leads her, in the magical language characteristic of the illustration, to want to be their fairy godmother, to rescue them from the horrors of their world. And it is only her that can be allowed to do this: it is clear early on that she is somewhat disdainful of the bourgeois morality of the children's foster home, despite the superficial signs of improvement in the children's behaviour and mood. The writer puts herself fully into the relationship with the children, encouraging them to show her their neediness and to be rescued. The result is that they explode – all their bad feelings come out in a barely controlled rage. In the writing, the worker copes with this by the use of a professional jargon which serves two principal functions. First, it operates as an emotional defence, protecting her against the rawness of the experience: the children are not attacking her but are 'acting out their feelings'. Second, the use of professional jargon redefines a course of action that originates in a personal desire to save the children, as an instance of professionalism: this is not just a struggle with two disturbed children, but an example of psychotherapy. In some ways, however, the jargon is a cover-up, rewriting history: apart from a generalised belief that it is good to express painful feelings (why?), there is no theoretical justification for the course that the intervention takes. What is actually a human, personal response to pain is expressed as a piece of work; what the writing reveals is that it is in fact adopting an image of the therapist as the dashing slayer of the dragon of all our nights.

The initial part of the therapist's account seeks to describe the picture of a family unable to cope without help – without the drastic 'help' entailed in the removal of the children, and the introduction not only of a substitute family, but also of herself as a social worker/therapist. The emotional deprivation is presented so forcibly that it obscures even the desire on the part of the reader to consider questions like, 'What is life like for this woman?', 'What would she require in order to manage with some degree of self-respect?' 'How and by whom has she been asked these and other related questions?' 'How does the therapist come to the conclusion that "these manifestations of disturbance in a child of seven were intolerable"', 'For whom was it intolerable – for Carol, the children, the worker, or the state?'. It is not that we cannot envisage a situation in which children need to be received into care, but we should at all times be clear and explicit as to our reasons. The very drama of this account, appealing as it does to our sense of caring and rescue, obscures the element of power and control, which are not only present in the decision to receive the children into care, but also in the therapeutic sessions themselves.

The worker talks about the need to 'renegotiate the balance of power', yet here under the guise of therapeutic process the whole question of power relations is avoided. The worker 'respects' the children by adopting a liberal view towards them: if you talk to people as people they will be reasonable. In this insistence on reasonableness, power relations are obscured. To put this another way, the author writes, 'I always felt it important to win their agreement'. Once again the issue of power is absent, as is the *process* by which the children choose, or are forced, to agree with the demands imposed on them by the adult.

Getting the children to relinquish their authority over the session is expressed as a therapeutic success. This raises problems for radical interventions: to what extent is the acceptance of controls a psychological advance as opposed to an exercise in increasing conformity? Towards the end of the account, the worker states that they 'also found the process of relinquishing their autocracy a little easier'. This is expressed as evidence of success, but is it? As radical therapists, should we not be encouraging a sense of power and anger? Autocracy implies selfishness; the use of this word may in some way be containing the worker's fear of the children and uncertainty over her actions – to say autocracy rather than power creates a safer role for her. The promotion of safety throughout the account is presented uncontentiously as an expression of the worker's concern for, and sensitivity towards, the trauma of these children's lives – for example, the account ends, '... which helped re-enter the world of school, from which they had taken an hour's respite'. The outside world is presented as something from which children need respite. The session is seen as the place of love and comfort, of experiences not attainable at home, school or elsewhere. The worker's feelings about the children and her role as fairy godmother obscure the fact that the session is both loving and painful – just like the outside world.

Illustration 3: Day Centre practice: therapy and tea-making

I want to write about therapeutic work in a psychiatric Day Centre. The Centre is described as an activity-based therapeutic community, which means that the therapeutic emphasis is on practical and creative groups and how they are approached, rather than on specifically verbally dynamic groups.

It seems most straightforward to look in detail at one collective activity which takes place regularly at the Centre. This activity is based on a practical task, making tea, which occurs during allotted informal periods in the course of a day at the Day Centre. Tea-making is one of a number of collective, practical tasks carried out at the Centre; others include preparing lunch, washing up, cleaning, and organising the weekly programme of activities. The good practice of these tasks is central to the smooth running of the Day Centre. The staff are expected to offer sensitive and thoughtful support towards the successful completion of these tasks, whilst they may often not participate directly in their execution.

I intend to describe a series of events relating to the making of tea and to comment on some of the processes which may have been taking place. One Friday, an incident took place at the Centre which, although seemingly trivial, had important consequences relating to the dynamics of the community. Just before lunchtime, one member (Jackie) arrived in the kitchen to make tea for herself and a small group of members who had been in a gardening group that morning. This provoked a considerable outburst from the group of members who were already in the kitchen preparing lunch. Their hostility was provoked partly by the fact that it was an unlawful activity to make tea at this time (according to one of the community rules), but also because the cooks had themselves tried to make tea earlier that morning, but couldn't find the tea. One of the cooks, Martha, accused Jackie of deliberately hiding the tea container, and much bad feeling was expressed between them. One result of this argument was that Jackie stated that in future she would buy her own tea and milk and would only make tea for herself at the Centre. This incident left a tense and difficult atmosphere in the Centre for the remainder of that Friday.

Although the tea incident was referred to in the large group meeting which took place on the Friday afternoon, it was not fully explored. This was partially owing to some of my anxieties at being the only staff member on duty that afternoon. There were other reasons, more easily justifiable to the community, for instance that there was not a very full complement of members present at this meeting. In addition, the meeting had other tasks and I felt some concern that this issue would not be clarified within the time available. Friday afternoon is usually a time for concluding the week, encouraging a drawing together of the community in preparation for the weekend, a period which most of the members find difficult. During the meeting, therefore, I suggested that the issues to do with tea-making could be more fully discussed at the next community meeting the following week. The community readily acquiesced in this proposal.

The next two days, following the weekend, there seemed to be less enthusiasm than was usual for the activities and tasks. On the day of the community meeting, most of the members opted to participate in a verbal discussion group. This was unusual, as less verbal groups were usually more popular. In fact, so many people wanted to take part in this group that it was necessary to split into two smaller groups. I participated in one of these groups, which elected to discuss the tea-making issue without any hesitation. Martha, who had been involved in Friday's incident, was also a member of this group.

An animated discussion took place, with numerous contributions from all group members. A consensus was reached by this group to reassert the ruling that members were not allowed to make tea outside the already designated times. The group also agreed that members who were cooking could continue to make themselves tea, as cooking was a particularly demanding and thirst-creating activity. It was also said in this group that the individual members who had held responsibility for collecting the tea money had gained excessive control over how and when the tea was made and whether there were any exceptions to the Centre rules. I learned that Jackie, a former tea money collector, had recently been in the habit of making tea for herself and her fellow gardeners at the end of the morning's activities. Until this point this breaking of the rule had not been mentioned by any other members either informally with a member of staff or formally in a group meeting.

It was agreed by most of the participants of this group that they had criticisms of the present tea money collector (who shall be called Thomas) regarding his attitude towards the task. Members expressed the view that he was harrassing, authoritarian and dictatorial. It was decided in this group that a more reliable (Thomas had occasional days away from the Centre) and less autocratic system would evolve if two members took equal responsibility for the job of collecting tea money. These points were put forward as proposals to bring to the afternoon's community meeting. The members of this small group also said that they would like me to take on a directive role in the community meeting. They argued that Thomas would feel less undermined by the changes in the system and in his responsibilities if I, rather than the members, laid out this new proposal. Before the discussion group finished, there was also a reference to members of staff who had preceded the existing staff team as being responsible for a stricter regime at the Centre, when meetings were held in an orderly fashion and members did as they were told.

That afternoon, the agenda was circulated as usual amongst the members and then reached the office for the staff to add any further items. I saw that no one had put tea-making on the agenda: this had been left for the staff to itemise and thus take responsibility for its introduction. In the meeting, I brought up the subject of tea-making as a difficult but central issue for the well-being of the community. I referred to the previous Friday's incident, and almost immediately Martha and Jackie re-engaged in their dispute. Voices became raised and angry recriminations were exchanged, including accusations of jealousy and trouble-making. Both Martha and Jackie expressed feelings of dislike, competition and rivalry relating to the organisation of the tea-making. The conflict and anger was intense, and several members looked towards the staff for reassurance or some kind of intervention in the dispute. The chairperson attempted to control the meeting and bring it to order. I sensed an expectation to contain or restrict the argument on behalf of the majority of the members, as several people were expressing considerable anxiety that the dispute should be brought to an end. I intervened in the argument by reminding the members from the discussion group of their various proposals. Some general discussion then took place, after which I suggested that the responsibility for collecting the tea money might rest more easily with two individuals sharing the task. Thomas spoke at this point, saying that he had no difficulty managing the tea money by himself and that he was quite satisfied with the present system. A further discussion then took place, with various individuals putting forward suggestions. The final result was that the community voted almost unanimously for Thomas to continue to take full responsibility for the tea money, but with a book to record payments in and a special tin for the money which would be kept at the Centre, rather than on his person as had previously been the case. It was agreed that another member would take over the job on days when Thomas was absent.

Comments on 'Therapy and tea-making'

The main issues in this piece arise from a complex set of distinctions which, in practice, either seem to conflict with each other or else to have a somewhat dubious rationale: client versus staff, old (authoritarian) versus new (democratic) styles of management, practical versus verbal therapy, the power of the author versus the collectivist ideology of the community, the management hierarchy outside versus the egalitarian ethos inside, rules versus individual liberty, democracy versus leadership. The author, as head of the Centre, its representative to the outside world and its leader, is at the centre of the contradictions generated by these oppositions, and it is this unstated and uncomfortable fact about her position that is at the heart of the piece.

The amusing juxtaposition of the title dismisses tea-making as apparently trivial, at the same time as tentatively asserting its importance as a shared activity in which members help and care for each other. However, the joke also makes us aware of an author who can stand outside 'Day Centre Practice' in order to make the joke, and it is this somewhat imaginary author who is outside and on top of the contradictions rather than subject to them that supposedly writes the piece. But the difficulty of maintaining this position is immediately apparent in the first paragraph: the 'I want' tries to assert the 'I' that is in charge, yet what follows is jargon-ridden, defensive, disclaimed even: 'The Centre is described as...' The idea that therapy can be practical rather than verbal is introduced, but the author is defensive: the alleged opposition between the practical and the verbal is surrounded by an excess of words ('specifically verbally dynamic groups'). Less 'verbal' Day Centres are lower down in the professional hierarchy, and defensiveness about the assumed devaluation of the Centre leads the author to propound a view she does not actually subscribe to: group/practical work is opposed to verbal/one-to-one relationship, but the reality is that both individual and group work goes on, some of which is verbal and some not, as witnessed by the discussion groups and community meetings that form the centre of the piece. The important point to stress here is perhaps not the specific contradictions that the author falls foul of, although of course there are important issues raised by the distinctions between group and individual activity and verbal and practical activity, but rather that this situation arises through the author's attempt to put herself in a position of certain, conscious knowledge of her experience when not actually in a position to do so – as shown by the way her language breaks down into confused jargon. This is compounded by the avoidance of one fact we can be sure of: that the author is head of the Centre, like it or not.

The cover-up, in relation to the readership, of the author's position has a parallel in the running of the Centre, where there is an ideology of openness, collective decision-making and egalitarianism which rather obscures both the clients' desire for a leader, as shown by the way the author is forced to take charge of the situation at critical points in meetings, and the author's leadership practice, which clearly has a crucial role in stopping the community from falling apart when seriously threatened by the conflict over tea-making. Political and moral principles, views on what is and what is not therapeutic, often seem to conflict, and the awkwardness this produces can easily lead to a cover-up of the power relations existing between patient/client/'member' and therapist. Real differences between them in outlook, the ability to express themselves, emotional integration, the ability to form relationships, live an independent life, cope with anxiety, become dissipated in the rosy idealised picture of the therapeutic collective. Rather than being therapeutic, this can have the effect of making it hard for both staff and clients to understand what is going on and thus deriving some benefit from their experience.

Turning to an examination of the incident described, it is interesting to note that despite the emphasis on the 'practical', as soon as the going gets hot the clients opt for discussion groups, and that in these groups the author is put under enormous pressure to take responsibility for making proposals and keeping the meeting in order, which she does. This is perhaps a measure of the strength of feeling stirred up by the conflict, as is the way the conflict is 'resolved' through a displacement on to Thomas. Everyone can agree on Thomas's poor performance, and this scapegoating offers a convenient way out of the explosive impasse of Martha and Jackie. This displacement occurs both in the discussion group and in the community meeting, ending with the unanimous vote that defuses the situation.

The incident is an illustration of the 'overdetermination' of any particular event by the convergence of many sets of forces that may be linked but operate on different levels. The tea-making incident could legitimately by viewed as a personality clash, a split between two groups, represented by Martha and Jackie respectively – these being more verbal members – a testing of the author's control and ability to contain conflict, or a clash between two management styles, the old and the new and, what may not be quite the same, the authoritarian and the democratic. None of these interpretations is exclusively correct, and to each must be added the effect of background factors such as the past history of the participants or the position of the Day Centre in the local management structure. Clearly, the issue in practice is at what level and in what manner to intervene. Whatever choices are made, it is essential for the worker to be able to think clearly about the factors involved, rather than just becoming part of a process that is beyond her/his control. The question thus arises of the theoretical framework and form of work organisation that would allow this to happen. Here it can be seen that while the author had little choice but to respond at the level of the anxiety being expressed, her position as Centre head is a vital element in the situation. Despite her power (or perhaps because of it) she appears as an isolated figure, caught between clients and an alien management structure, with little source of support or constructive sharing of her experience. There is an obvious need for a work practice that enables this experience to be understood as a function of her situation, rather than being due simply to 'personal' strengths or weaknesses.

Finally, this illustration shows dramatically the power of the forces at work in groups and the effect of fear of disintegration on staff, clients and management structure. That these forces become manifest at times of crisis does not mean that they do not operate the whole time, constantly limiting the horizons of a group's thought and activity. This will apply to any work group, highlighting the need for an understanding of group processes rather than a set of postulates which states that groups should function in this or that way, for example as democratic or leaderless. Such an understanding would be relevant to any working group, whether involved in therapy or political campaigning.

Summary of issues from 'Therapy and personal change' illustrations

One striking characteristic of all three illustrations in this section is the defensiveness of the way they are written. Each author apologises for making judgements or writing the piece at all, 'therapeutic' jargon is commonly used to obscure the immediacy of the events that are being described, or extraneous arguments are introduced to distract attention from the central processes. At least two of the three authors attempt to write themselves out the story, and none of them are able to state with confidence the principles upon which they are basing either their actions or their words. What anxieties could this defensiveness be defending against? From the analyses of the pieces, two major explanations have arisen: power and feeling.

All three illustrations are built on a more or less common model of radical acceptability, which involves being non-judgemental, non-controlling to the point of libertarianism, of being reasonable, sympathetic and democratic. The problem with this is that, based as it is on the 'rational' model of humanness that we have criticised in earlier chapters, it has rather little to do with what is actually happening in each of the examples. The events are not reasonable, the protagonists are not brought together through a mutual contractual obligation that is fulfilled through conscious, polite procedures, nor are therapists and clients possessed of equal power, in the crudest as well as the most sophisticated senses of that word. This last issue is the most central: all three illustrations confront issues of power head on, yet only in Illustration 1 is there any recognition that power relations have been systematically exploited. The failure to deal with power issues is the most curious and widespread problem posed by the illustrations. It is as if power is identified with oppression and hence is inadmissible in the work of politically conscious therapists; its presence is therefore denied even when it is most obviously at the centre of events. Any possible positive functions of power are left unconsidered, despite the apparent therapeutic efficacy of some of the clearest instances of personal assertion, especially in the first two illustrations. It is as if the authors are so uncomfortable with the idea of their influence on their clients that they prefer to pretend that nothing special is occurring. There are two immediate consequences of this situation. First, in the interests of presenting themselves as politically acceptable therapists, the authors have actually written politics out of their accounts: without considering power relations one can never grasp political relations. Second, the denial that power relations are central to the personal encounters of therapy means that the actual events that are experienced, more particularly their psychodynamic determinants, are obscured by a defensive smokescreen which leaves everything liberal, reasonable and innocuous. It is here that the politics of therapy presents itself forcefully. These illustrations, despite standing aside from political explicitness, contain political values which are possibly more influential through being obscured, and which are not necessarily consistent with the positions the authors would like to adopt. Power is used, both therapeutically and defensively; by covering up the centrality of power relations the authors communicate their unease with this apparent challenge to their egalitarian self-image. This suggests an uncertainty about the positions they hold, a reluctance to lead or to become definite in their therapeutic relationships, an inability to state clearly in action the direction in which their politics might take them. It is clearly easier to labour under the fantasy that people can be liberated simply by being cared for (a liberal fantasy) than to confront the power issues that raise their heads.

The second explanation for the defensiveness of the three illustrations is shown most clearly in Illustration 3: the anxieties generated by the intensity of the clients' distress are personally threatening to the therapists. All three authors are uncomfortable with such intensity. The first author takes refuge by playing down the relational context of the therapy, thus making himself disappear to such an extent that the therapeutic effects of his interpretations gain a magical flavour. In addition, there is a persecutory flavour to some of these interpretations which is not lost on the client and which presumably has its source in the author's own unease. The second author copes mainly by the imposition of social work/therapeutic jargon on the raw experience of confrontation with the children: what might be interpreted as an assault on a persecuting adult by two pained and deprived youngsters becomes instead an interesting example of play therapy carried out by a professional. The third author writes her responses out of the tale, fails to spot the displacement of anxiety on to a scapegoat, and belittles the significance of 'dynamic' as opposed to 'practical' interventions in the face of an extremely anguished psychodynamic encounter. In all three illustrations, the implicit model is that identified in the discussion of power: there is personal pain, certainly, and therapeutic skill; the measured, rational application of the one will in the end appease the other. Our argument is that the true politics of the therapeutic situation resides in its unpredictable, unspoken, awkward bits, the bits that are not rational, 'correct' or under control.

THERAPY AND STRUGGLE

Illustration 4: the Children's Home group

This example explores the links between personal change and political action by focusing on a group of workers in an intensive residential caring setting – a staff group in a Children's Home run by a social services department. Children in this Home could be admitted at very short notice and stay for anything up to about six months. Thus the staff were faced with a changing population of sometimes very distressed children with whom the possibilities for 'therapeutic' work were limited by the brevity and uncertainty of their stay. Within the Home there was a Head (Robert) and two deputies (Alice and Ruth); the rest of the staff was made up of houseparents working in pairs. Staff members were in general quite young and poorly paid; they worked shifts which played havoc with their lives outside the Home, and on the whole they received little training or professional support. I originally became involved with the Home when I met the two deputies by accident and offered to help them out by advising them on the management of individual children. This offer was taken up and for a year we had weekly group sessions to discuss ways of dealing with the children in the Home. In the second year of my involvement the group changed to something the staff called a 'sensitivity group', focusing on the relationships between staff members rather than on the children. In fact, throughout a year of weekly group meetings children were barely mentioned, although staff sometimes justified the time given to the group by stating that the way workers got on with one another was important for the way they handled the children. The change in the group, from discussion to 'sensitivity', came about following a traumatic encounter between Robert and one of his houseparents (Jill) which led to a summer of upheaval and discontent in the Home. At the end of that time the staff decided to try out the 'sensitivity group' idea and asked me to sit in on it because, they said, they trusted me to be able to provide a reasonably balanced outsider's viewpoint on what was going on. At the end of the second year, I decided to stop leading the group, partly because I felt that I had become so involved with the staff that it was proving increasingly difficult for me to provide the 'outsider's challenge' that they needed.

The group developed in fits and starts, with themes begun one week disappearing and then cropping up again several weeks later. Many of the sessions were very tense, leaving me feeling emotionally drained at the end, and unsure of whether I'd been able to pull together all the many strands of the events that had taken place. In this account, I am going to focus on three sessions which seem to me to demonstrate the major themes of the group's development, and which raise for consideration questions about the impact of the group on workers' personal relations and feelings, as well as on their work, and the relationship between the political events that affected the Home and the functioning of the group. The examples also demonstrate two different aspects of my involvement with the group: firstly, a distanced, commentating attitude trying to make sense of things; secondly, a more involved posture of identification with the group in its struggles. I am going to present the important parts of these sessions without much comment, in the form they take in the notes that I wrote immediately after each session. All names are changed.

The first incident that I want to describe came in the fourth session of the group and served as a kind of 'founding myth', to which people referred back on several occasions, usually when they wanted to make a statement about how important the group was or about how successfully people usually hid their feelings from one another. The previous week, Alice had come under attack, particularly from Jill, who accused her of

not supporting the Union in its complaints against management practices, and of diverting energy away from militant
action by acting as an emotional carrier, taking on everyone's
angry feelings. The next session started with a great deal of
tension: it was clear that there'd been several incidents with Jill
during the week and that some people had come to the group
intending to confront her, only to find that she had pre-
empted them by deciding to leave the group. This had always
been preserved as an option, and as another rule was that
people didn't talk about others not present in the group, many
people felt angry and frustrated. Alice was particularly upset.

Alice said that she'd been confused at the end of the
previous session, and had come prepared to pick it up with
Jill. Now she felt thwarted and vulnerable, but she had four
days' break coming and was going to use that time to think
through what she should do. She seemed quite tearful, but
there was little response: Robert touched her momentarily
and Ruth said that she realised that everyone had been feeling
the tension and had been going to Alice to talk about it with
her. Sylvia said how she admired Alice's ability to cope, and
others agreed that they would always go to her for help. Alice
said that although she was feeling confused, she was nevertheless confident that she could cope with things, especially with
taking on other people's feelings. I said that it seemed to be
important to everyone that Alice could cope, but that I was
worried about her, that she seemed fragile to me and that I
didn't think she really could cope at all. At this, Alice burst
into tears and sobbed for some minutes, while Jack, Andy and
Marie cuddled her and gave her attention and everyone else
looked on, very upset. Alice said I'd 'hit the nail on the head',
and told everyone that she felt she'd been giving and giving all
through her three years at the Home and had never taken
from anyone, and that she couldn't manage anymore – so
much so that she'd arranged to see a therapist to help her cope
with work. The others agreed that they went to her as a kind
of reflex when anything went wrong – 'pouring shit down a
toilet'. People all were talking in terms of Alice needing to
learn to take more for herself from others: I pointed this out
and suggested they were still putting the onus for change on
her, not on themselves.

Alice's central position in the emotional life of the Home was constant throughout the group sessions – the 'mother' who could hold herself together enough to take on everyone else's unhappiness. This session, however, marked an important point in alerting the group to Alice's role, and in starting to reveal the extent of unease that was bubbling beneath the surface of the Home.

As the incident with Alice reveals, the group often functioned by denying the extent of disagreements or problems, only to have them explode when some external event placed pressure on everyone. The two other examples that I want to give showed this very clearly in practice, and also reveal how difficult I found it to maintain the traditional distance of a group leader. Both these incidents have to do with politics, in different senses of the word.

About midway through the year, there were a number of management moves in the borough which resulted in a threat of industrial action which would leave the Home unattended, possibly putting the children at risk in a way that would have been intolerable to some members of staff. When we met for the group, there was a brief, very tense silence, which I broke by asking how the week had been. Jack said it had been mainly tense because of the threat of industrial action. At the Union meeting the previous week he'd been unable to see other people's points of view, and had been frustrated by his inability to persuade people to his own position. Alice described a lot of the tension as being over leaving the kids if action was called for, something she was unwilling to do. I asked if Alice had been isolated over this issue, but she hadn't been. I suggested that what was happening was that the anger and frustration felt towards management was somehow, because of the impotence of their position, being vented on one another and that this was analogous to other industrial conflicts where managment exploits splits in the workforce – in this case the lever was the guilt felt over the children. Jack talked about how the lack of autonomy led to frustration, and how when staff came face to face with their powerlessness in certain situations they stopped looking at them. There was a silence, so I asked if this was another situation they weren't looking at. Immediately, an animated discussion broke out as

Jack pointed out that Robert, Alice and Ruth got a lot of stick because of their midway position between workers and mangement. Expression of feelings about the difficulty of their role led to a showdown between Andy and Alice: Andy conveyed that he didn't trust Alice to stand up to management pressures. Alice became very angry, demanding to know what Andy thought of her, asserting that she was 'one hundred per cent' behind the Union. Andy backtracked, and I summarised by returning to the importance of attending to the splits among workers which made them weaker when fighting management.

This session revealed how, when faced with outside pressures and a consciousness of powerlessness, the group split: individuals became tense with one another because of their failure at persuasion, the hierarchy in the Home became beleaguered and the object of suspicion; most of all, people lost their trust in one another and their sense of solidarity, believing that in the end they would stand alone, exposed by other people's failure to act.

The second major event which exposed underlying group emotions came when one of the workers (Andy) was sent to prison for three years for his part in a picket that had occurred a year previously. Although everyone had known that his case was coming up for trial, Andy had made most people think that he would get off, and his arrest and possible conviction had never been talked about within the group. Outside group sessions, one worker (Jill) had known how afraid Andy was that he might get sent down, but Robert and Alice, who had supervised Andy's work, had been convinced by him that he had good evidence on his side. In the event, his only defence had been that he couldn't remember what had happened during the picket. The day after Andy was sentenced, I went to the Home to run a group to find everyone in a state of shock, acting as if a sudden death had occurred. Everyone was completely convinced of Andy's innocence, and there was a great deal of anger directed at the police but also at the group – particularly from Jill, who felt that nobody had been willing to help Andy talk about his fears. There was also a strong feeling of guilt, as people thought they had not provided Andy with the support he needed. Only Janet stood outside this, angry at Andy for what she saw as his stupidity and resenting the attention he was getting for this, although the prevailing feelings in the Home made it difficult for her to express herself in this way. My role over this time was to attempt to counsel and support people individually, as well as to encourage the 'mourning' element in the group's functioning. I also made links between the failure to discuss and prepare for Andy's sentence and other denials made in the group. It was clear that there were still a lot of strong feelings about the violence that had been perpetrated on Andy and about the group's failure to deal with the issues, and these came to a head four weeks after the sentence.

At the beginning of the session Jill, who had returned to the group, had been saying that there were a lot of separations taking place in the Home, and I had noted the very tense emotional climate. There'd also been some discussion of what had happened to Andy. I was feeling agitated about Alice, who'd been silent throughout. I asked her if she was angry and she said 'steaming', but it was 'too near the surface' for her to talk about it. There was a silence and then Jill said that Alice terrified her, because she thought that Alice's anger was directed at her. Alice said her anger was 'all over the place', but especially directed at Andy: she'd supported him and really tried with him, and she'd been shocked when it turned out that his only defence was that he 'couldn't remember'. After some talk about whether such amnesia was possible, Jill said that she didn't want to hear a re-run of the trial, but just saw it as being about the group. Janet then came in to say that she felt angry at Andy for all the attention he was getting. Jill said that 'as usual' Janet was defending herself behind generalities, so Janet said this was right: 'as everyone knew', she was jealous because of Jill's 'infatuation' with Andy. Jill became angry at being 'patronised', and rowed with Janet, becoming more upset and aggressive, and accusing the group of being untrustworthy. She also attacked Alice for saying that Jill couldn't allow herself to trust the group. Jill agreed that her feelings over Andy were tied up in what was going on, but said that she felt criticised whatever she did. Marie got drawn into this, saying that she really disagreed with Jill, that people in the group had tried very hard, and that the group couldn't be expected to do everything. A violent argument then broke out between Marie and Jill, much of it having to do with Marie's relationship with another woman in the Home. Marie had in turn long harboured resentments over Jill's 'rejection' of her. Jill claimed that she couldn't be 'false', which was interpreted by others as implicitly criticising the rest of the group for avoiding truths. The rest of the group was angry and silent, or became dragged into an impotent mediating role. The session ended very late.

The following week, the events of this session were explored in a much calmer atmosphere, with several people saying that they shared the anger with Andy which Alice had expressed, and with a recognition of the difficult time that there'd been in the Home. Several people paid tribute to one another's abilities in keeping going, with particular praise for the way Alice had once again held everyone together. Alice said that this might be so, but she didn't feel strong – she couldn't always take on everyone's feelings anymore. The material brought up by the conviction of Andy and the events that followed in the Home were never completely resolved, and resulted in Jill leaving the Home with considerable tension surrounding her. The experiences of that time did have some positive effects on the group: it ceased to be possible for people to defend themselves against difficult issues by distinguishing between 'personal' and 'work' life – the two were intertwined to an inseparable degree. It also brought to the fore the functions and dangers of defences, motivating group members to investigate more fully the events of the Home. It mobilised the anger against external oppressive political forces, particularly management, to some degree and helped set the ground for more solidarity over later issues.

Comments on 'The Children's Home group'

This account raises many issues: the dilemmas of being a residential worker; the need for supervision in social work; problems of team work and the effects of hierarchical structures and group dynamics, as well as its stated aim of 'exploring the links between personal change and political action'. These issues conceal what are, for us, crucial dilemmas in the pursuit of a more radical practice. The piece throws up an enormous amount of confusion around leadership and power, including the difficulty of using therapeutic skills and political leadership as means of furthering our radical practice. Socialists have always tended oversimplistically to link power with control, domination and oppression, and as a result have been unable to exploit fully the potential for influencing change in a simultaneously therapeutic and political sense. This kind of confusion about the liberating and oppressive aspects of power are often acted out and experienced as lack of clarity about roles and boundaries. It is very common, for example, for radical mental health workers to be active trade unionists, at the same time as being conscientious skilled professionals, without finding ways to analyse and begin to bridge this split. The result is often confused, individualised thinking and responding: a liberal practice which in the end fails to be subversive. Exploring these kinds of contradictions and conflicts had led us to the conclusion that evading issues of power, whether they be statutory, therapeutic or those of class privilege, can, as in this example, lead to a need to withdraw rather than an ability to facilitate change and exert wider spheres of influence. This example is important in that it provides us with a context of primarily personal change, and yet the worker is also faced with a situation where he can potentially help his clients to act as political beings as well. This raises issues of helping people to care for themselves, for each other and, in a wider sense, for the service they are providing.

One of the main areas of confusion throughout the piece seems to be the lack of clarity about what the group is for, and a consequent lack of delineation of the role and function of the worker-therapist-facilitator. The staff clearly felt guilty about their needs and used a defensive strategy to try and justify the group in social work terms. At the same time they were also ambivalent about seeking a leader but seemed to be asking for an 'outsider's challenge' which the worker describes as 'a distanced, commentating attitude'. The difficulty involved in resolving these issues from the start (was this largely down to fear of rejection and/or fear of commitment?) left the worker in a situation where he felt he not only took responsibility for making links and interpretations for the group, but also for encouraging ventilation and containing a lot of painful, 'messy' feelings; and, crucially, at the same time he was concealing his leadership role, he was maintaining the fiction that the group was a democratic one. This contradiction led to major problems for both the group and the worker, who suffered discomfort and overloading which he describes as feeling 'emotionally drained' and 'unsure'. The omission of exploring the positive as well as the negative aspects of leadership and power drains away a significant amount of his energy and skill. On the one hand, in a liberal sense he has attempted to drop the oppressive aspects of leadership, by, we assume, being approachable, friendly, accepting, perhaps even overtly expressing left-wing views. At the same time, however, he is leaving himself and the group unprotected by also dropping the potentially liberating aspects of his position as group leader. He therefore more easily gets drawn into their complex intermeshing of relationships, which ultimately leaves him caring enormously about the individuals but disempowered as a therapist to help them either with their dynamics or with their political dilemmas in the outside world.

We have exposed, then, the worker's difficulty in exploring the positive and radical potential of acknowledging and using power. It also needs to be emphasised how this kind of concealment tends to hide other processes and factors. The group, for example, denies it has a leader, but they invite one in; additionally they deny they are part of a management structure even within their own staff group, and yet they are suspicious of management and each other. Through ventilation and underlying analysis of feelings and conflicts, some of their defensive strategies are revealed and worked on. We are aware that this kind of exploration needs an atmosphere of safety and trust, and one of the most necessary components for this is the setting up of clear boundaries, roles and limits to work within. Again, as socialists we have a tendency to deny difference, so strongly do we believe in equality of opportunity. Contradictory as it may seem, emphasis and understanding of the differences, for example between the leader and the group, can result in a greater ability to analyse what the power relationships really are, and therefore increased potential to act and struggle in the real world. Similarly, in working with working-class clients, emphasising the differences between them and the worker can lead to an enormous amount of envy and anger, which none of us find easy. Nevertheless, it is these very feelings that are often the basis for action, and by acknowledging them we are more likely to help them be directed more fruitfully at a political target, rather than at just an individual one.

One of the most obvious reflections of the worker's ambivalence about his position of power is the way he has almost completely edited himself out of the exposition. Not only does this undermine the real centrality of his position and his importance in the group, but it also encourages the myth of the magic element in therapy and change. Because we cannot rely on the author's description of his own experience during the course of the work, it is easy to fantasise that his maturity and skill were enormously helpful and almost spiritual – take, for example, his ability to 'hit the nail on the head' with no preamble as to the evidence and feelings of his own, which he must have used to make any worthwhile interpretation.

The most difficult aspect of this process to grapple with seems to be that part which involves overt political actions and decisions in a wider sphere. In this group they are faced with seeing themselves as carers of vulnerable children who are dependent on them, which feels discrepant with themselves as workers struggling politically against their management structure. This issue is further highlighted by the fact that the group itself is a hierarchical one. The members of the group experienced these parts of themselves as irreconcilable and contradictory, and this seemed to be acted out as a reflection in the group, in which the author also seemed to experience his different roles as leader and radical worker as discrepant. An exposé of the latter may well have facilitated resolution of the former dilemmas for the group concerned. The strength of established ideology and practice within a group is immense. All roles and social behaviour tend to lead to the denial of conflict and the preservation of the group. A major threat is experienced in this group, for example by the fact of different sexual relationships taking place between some members of the group. The strength of this is so vivid that the author himself reproduces the reticence in his written piece, the relationships are hinted at rather than open facts for all to know and face up to. Uncomfortable and conflictual feelings left unanalysed retain their power to split the group, and are then experienced as dangerous and very threatening. Additionally, their creative function is swamped and forgotten.

In conclusion this piece is a perfect example of unconscious feelings having the power to drain away the energy and therefore the radical potential of a group to act in the outside world. It further elaborates the idea that political, therapeutic practice is not just a matter of having the correct socialist perspective at the time; it also involves an exposure and analysis of underlying and often unconscious feelings and conflicts.

Illustration 5: Racial awareness training for social workers

Gradually twenty or so social workers came to the room. For some this is just another seminar, for others there is the anxiety about how this session might make them feel. For a few, the black students, there is on the one hand scepticism about how far Racial Awareness Training is relevant to them, and, on the other hand, the nagging doubt as to whether whites really want to be anti-racist.

An anti-racist rhetoric is by now well established. There have been films, lectures and discussions, on the history of racism, on imperialism, on the structural position of blacks, their experience as workers in the inherently racist institutions, and on the need for struggle. This course has the clear objective of change. It is based on the view that ideas inform practice, which in turn develops/modifies ideas. Racial Awareness Training develops the rhetorical stance by exploring what inhibits an anti-racist practice. It is not in conflict with a structural analysis, but seeks to add to it by looking at those inhibitions that are within us as people.

The session begins. I explain that the objectives are to share openly our experience of confronting racism, and to learn from each other: not with a view to producing guilt, or competition about who is most 'right-on', but rather to consider how and why we act as we do... (or don't). Rather than have an anecdotal session, we agree upon a role play, which is just as well as I had one prepared. I know that consent is, at least in part, a consequence of the power relations between us. I am aware of the fact that it is tempting as a teacher to imply that I have already met and overcome the problems of being anti-racist, which, of course, I haven't. Six volunteers leave the room. I give out roles with the instructions not to discuss them with the others.

The scene is a café. A queue forms behind a rather indecisive person who wants their egg done on both sides, a black coffee with sugar, and, oh yes, a glass of water and a slice of bread. The next person brusquely goes up to the counter asks for tea-to-go and a sandwich. 'That will be 63p. Have you any smaller change? I am rather short'. 'No I bloody well haven't... I said I wanted my sandwich in a bag, and keep your fucking black hands off my food'. The waitress looks frightened as he storms out leaving his tea.

The role play ends, the whole incident took no more than a few minutes. There is silence in the room as the 'actors' sit down. There was a distinctly uneasy atmosphere in the room: 'How do we talk about what we have just seen?' Watching what we don't want to see arouses deep feelings, uncomfortable feelings which range from resentment towards the role play: 'It's artificial, it's not like real life' (and inevitably resentment towards me for suggesting the exercise) to anger and shock. Furthermore, watching with others is in itself threatening, with its implicit requirement that we account for what we see and how we act. It makes public that which we prefer to keep private. 'It occurs to me', says one of the students,' that I never talk about the racist incidents that I see, I certainly never in general conversation consider either what I should have done or how it affects *me*'. The difficulty we are facing, then, is that we are used to externalising the problem. It is in effect 'something other people do, somebody else's problem'.

A black student says, 'All white people are racist, *you*, not us, are the problem'. Being part of the problem is hard for white 'liberals' to take on. It is easier to see the cause of racism as a product of the socio-economic relations of capitalism, unemployment or the cuts. It is easier to be in opposition, to identify with the oppressed as women, as gays, as the disabled, as the unemployed, or to be against the bomb. To be part of the problem that is much more difficult. The education, culture, institutions and the consequent socialisation of white people are essentially racist. Resistance to change (to the active adoption of an anti-racist position) arises from the internalisation of privilege, which is not only of material benefit, but is also concerned with power. Racism is part of ourselves as white people.

The stunned silence that followed the role play was in part a response to the violence of the encounter; 'I was really surprised at how frightening I found it'; 'I never realised how brutalising such "small" incidents were'. The role play gave an insight into events that black people experience daily, experiences that are all too often trivialized: 'It is really important to keep a sense of proportion and not to overreact'. 'It is really important not to let these incidents make you bitter.' Just as children must accept the often unpredictable, arbitrary and brutal experience of school life as part of their maturation, so by implication must blacks rise above their experience irrespective of its nature. The unconscious racist association between blacks and children is extremely powerful – 'it takes time for them to learn our culture and our ways' – and has the effect of creating the conditions whereby the authenticity of black experience can be overlooked, which in turn avoids the necessity of criticising those forces that determine the experience. Just as children are seen as irrational, demanding and subversive, so blacks, consistent with the historical view of them as sub-human (and certainly not adults) are required to learn from their oppression. Here the analogy breaks down, since for children the prize of learning is acceptance into the adult world; for blacks they must stay as children.

The fiction of being a reasonable person in a reasonable society is compelling. The unreasonableness of the racist abuse on the waitress was blatant: 'I felt sorry for the waitress, I wanted to support her'; 'You could see how powerless she felt, almost resigned in fact'; '...but it was good that she didn't answer back, that would have demeaned her'. Pity and concern for the waitress led with some obvious relief to a discussion about how best she should conduct herself, and how we could support her. The process was obvious; on the one hand we could demonstrate how caring we were, and on the other we could distance ourselves from the problem. The discussion would have continued in this way had somebody not said 'I realise that I always help people after the event, I never really consider the event itself'. We were forced to confront the issue of our passivity. At least to confront the question we had been so assiduously avoiding: 'What could we have done in the café, and how could we confront racism rather than just comfort the victim?'

The issue seemed to be how to use our anger. In the role play nobody acted, nobody moved. It was as if we were mesmerised by the violence and irrationality of the act. Is anger so contaminating that to 'react' in anger is to render us essentially no different from the racist?

There was then a powerful injection against action, against change. In part this was due to the fear of having to act alone, and not being able to be certain of those around us, but also it reflected how ideological socialisation is. The dominant reactions of shock and pity would generally be applauded as humane, but they are inescapably conservative – they are a defence against the legitimate feelings of injustice, outrage and anger, which are the motivating forces for action and change. The association between strong feelings and irrationality is a major inhibition which needs to be confronted as a precondition for both individual and collective action.

Comments on 'Racial awareness training for social workers'

This piece describes a wide range of challenges that are raised within a practical workshop on the experience of racism in everyday life. Some of these challenges arise from the relationship between such an experiment and its wider political framework, and some from the individual participant's responses when confronted with the issue of how to act or react. The first of these challenges centres on the word 'practical': the author's advocacy of personal experience as the only way to confront an internalised racist ideology. Lectures, seminars and the like are clearly worthy, but in the absence of experience can lead simply to 'rhetoric'. The workshop is presented as a first attempt at exposing these helping-profession students to the personal reality of racism, the implicit statement, endorsing an intellect/experience dichotomy, being that only experiential work can really teach political lessons, that if awareness is to amount to more than just making the right noises, it has to merge with personal change. While the strength of this argument is revealed in the example, it is by no means unproblematic: difficulties arise, for instance, in considering the mechanics of the 'learning' that goes on in the session as well as the wider politics of the 'personal change'.

In this racial awareness exercise there are both black and white participants, and the group leader is white. Under most circumstances this would be an issue around which much confrontation ('learning'?) would centre – for example, in the analogous situation of a man running a mixed group on sexism. Surprisingly, the author of the illustration refers to no tension about this within the group and does not reveal whether the ensuing discussion brought the group together or forced its black and white members apart. Given the reliance on personal experience, this is an extraordinary state of affairs. Its essence, perhaps, can be found in his phrase 'to learn from each other'. The author tells his students that he has as much to learn as they do (which, as he is white, is clearly the case), that the process will be democratic, but that he has clear ideas of what he wants. It is possible that this somewhat fictitious democracy is paralleled by a fictitious readiness to learn: can confronting one's own racism be more than play-acting within the structures of a social work training course? More strongly, it is not clear that everyone who attends a course like this as part of their training as a 'helping professional' really wants to learn in the sense advocated by the author – a painful and threatening encounter with unpleasant parts of oneself. Although the role-play encounter is moving and powerful, its limits are severe; the whole situation has the reassuring structure of play, with the safe grounding of the white leader ensuring that anything too threatening can be woken up from, that daddy will protect us from the terrors of the dark. There is no description of a real (in the group) black–white encounter because this is not reality; despite the claim of democracy and the apparent willingness to be part of the group, the author retains control, as leader and safety net. A thought that arises here is whether this kind of play, shared by therapeutic encounters as well as 'learning' ones, is necessary for personal change, and whether, if this is so, it reveals the distance between therapy and political action.

The role-play of events in the café bring up a number of dilemmas for the group. Underlying their personal doubts is clearly some anxiety about whether they are in a position to do anything at all, as well as about the sources of their inactivity. But it is in dealing with the feelings that arise in the group that the piece is at its most interesting. 'Watching what we don't want to see arouses deep feelings', writes the author, listing resentment, anger and shock. Yet the feelings that are described are not necessarily all that deep, although they do demonstrate that people have been moved by the experience. Some of them may be 'replacement' feelings in two senses, either substituting resentment of the role play for a response to it, or reacting in a socially predictable manner. The problem is that it is often difficult to distinguish 'artificial' feelings of this kind from deep, 'real' ones. As such, feelings such as 'shock' can sometimes be the reasonable, liberal response which shows the individual's humanity without challenging her/his personality. It is interesting that the author assures us of the 'depth' of the feelings expressed without raising these points. The expository tone of this section links with a recurrent attribute of this illustration, which is the author's mistrust of the reader's ability to interpret the raw material of the participants' responses. Instead, everything is described with a commentary, to ensure that we understand its implications and its roots. Perhaps the 'I have seen the light' flavour that results reflects again the author's ambiguous position as a white teacher leading a workshop on racism for black and white students. He attempts to forestall criticism by earnestness, commitment, and repetitive reference to how 'racism is part of ourselves' (prejudging, perhaps, who the 'us' reading the piece will be); in so doing, he communicates a sense of unease, as if the material relating to the workshop is too dangerous to describe without comment. The varying and uncertain uses of the words 'we' and 'our' here and through-out the illustration reflect the author's uncertainty over his own position: he is leader, interpreter and activist, identifying simultaneously with oppressor and oppressed. The personality of the author enters in this way into what is on the surface a highly politicised account, partially obscuring the politics of the situation but also revealing the sense in which it is really entwined with personal change.

Illustration 6: Political therapy group

Our label is a clear one: we are a socialist feminist group; our struggles, direction and our dynamic life as a group are far more confused than our name. The socialist spectrum amongst us is wide, as is the feminist; nevertheless our common concerns are far greater than our differences. We desire and believe in the necessity, as women, to be in a women-only environment for at least this space and time once a week, to struggle, to grow and to help each other and find the strength to fight. We aim to analyse the world around us as socialists and feminists, and therefore to act differently both in groups and individually, both politically and personally. The group for us is not only an alternative family, and a political group which analyses and acts in the outside world, it is also a place where we can explore our inner worlds, our deep and strong feelings which all too often lead us to behave in ways which contradict our beliefs and ideals. We all share both a history of frustration with male-dominated political parties, and also situations where much if not most of our energy was being drawn into struggle with our own comrades rather than into the struggle against the state (i.e. our original target). We also shared a frustration and hopelessness about changing ourselves, a confusion and uncertainty about where to go after 'understanding' our position as women. We all wanted to find ways to feel differently and behave differently. Our aims are really very grand: to exclude neither the political nor the personal but to include them in our arena simul-taneously.

There are ten of us in the group. We have been meeting for five years. In that time we have changed and moved in many directions; we have each had changing needs and in different ways we have tried to fulfil them all. Of course we have both succeeded and failed. We are all joined in wanting the group to continue. We argue and compromise. We are all very committed. One evening a week from eight till late, until we finish. As the evening gets late, very late, we are either rivetted by what we have created together and we don't want to leave, each woman having to return to her separate home, or else we are fixed by disappointment, having been locked in disagreement (sometimes silent) on how to use our time. Each of these alternatives tell a similar story; we are aware of our power as a group of women, our ability and potential to move each other on, to challenge fear and 'stuckness' and fight the inequalities that we see and experience in the world, by joining with greater and greater numbers of women. We also know we can abuse this very same power which helps us to understand one another, by sympathising, empathising, but fearing confrontation and criticism, we can often fail to take the necessary steps for change. We disappoint each other, some of us love each other. We sometimes become a complex, interwoven network of each other's families, and sometimes we break free. It is nearly always an uneasy mixture of comfort and struggle.

I cannot represent five years in a short description; I have chosen parts of our experience together in the hope that these may somehow be representative.

Sexuality. We weren't even sure at the start what the word meant. When we were children we used to look in the dictionary for anwers to questions that we couldn't put into words. In the group we started tentatively finding our questions together. We began with coloured crayons and drew our bodies, the head first, then neck, then shoulders, etc. For each part of our bodies we thought of an object, an animal, a shape or a colour. Our self-images were monstrous, some thin, hard and wiry, others messy, huge masses of flesh, almost glutinous. We all hated some of the bits of our bodies, failing to see them as a whole, having done imaginary self-dismembering and dismantling on a million occasions. We moved on. We shared the dark terror of the first day of our periods, as well as the blood. We shared our mothers and the tears and the shame. We grew to know each other as sisters and as daughters. We went over our first experiences of sex, classroom touching, playground guilt. All the feelings came flooding back, at times we were rigid with embarrassment and at others silent with fear. We split into pairs and took ten minutes each way. We sat facing our partners – some of us held hands, for others even that was too hard. We took it in turns to be 'counsellor' and 'client', the former keeping eye contact and only intervening along the lines of "try repeating that" or "how did that feel?" and making sure not to interrupt, ask for explanation, judge or offer solutions. The 'client' talked aloud about all the incidents and feelings she could remember on the theme of masturbation, my first sexual experience, my genitals, etc. We found that one incident or memory loomed larger than the others and we tried to give each of us the time to explore the issue which was most difficult. We found that our heads were full of 'shoulds' and 'shouldn'ts', like 'I should be clean', 'I should fancy my husband', 'I shouldn't want sex with strangers', 'Every time I look at an advert I feel it's telling me I should be beautiful'. We got angry together and excited. The meetings went on very, very late. Then we got stuck. We moaned and moaned about our lot in life as women and we didn't like ourselves. We forgot about change, we must have felt very scared. Then we realised we had set up an alternative set of oughts – a Liberated Superego or an ABC of How to be Liberated. It was better to be a lesbian or celibate then to be heterosexual; it was better to have had a lesbian experience or to want to than not to have had one, or not to want to; it was better to have more than one sexual relationship than to just have one; it was better to be non-possessive than to be jealous and possessive. Our new list was as endless as our old one, and we were using the same threads of the web, although the pattern of capture was different. We tried to start again and listen to each other's feelings, really understand that each woman's starting place was different and her journey long and slow needed encouragement and support as well as criticism. We were all so used to being rated, we had taken over the task and were subtly but determinedly boxing each other in. We started to move away from labels then, slowly though, and onto the issues which were then freer to surface with less fear of ridicule and failure. As it stands we often compete with each other, feel smug or outcast according to where we come on the shoulds and shouldn't scale of how we feel and what we do. The difference is we are increasingly aware and challenge each other for remarks designed to compete, put down or label without exploration. It often feels as if we are getting nowhere, the overall progress is so slow. We are painfully learning how to go about learning – how to change.

There came a time when we had to acknowledge that we were unable to touch each other physically (most of us had even withdrawn in this way from our mothers). Verbally we explored some of the deepest crevices and yet holding hands was embarrassing and painful. We touched our lovers and our children, but those of us who were childless and also without a sexual relationship had to, on the whole, negotiate life without the warmth and 'holding' that touch provides. We wanted to cross this boundary, to expand the ways in which we could be close to each other, to more fully use our bodies for expression and fulfilment, and overcome inhibitions which felt limiting. We also had ideological aims to cross these barriers as women together – to look to each other for things that we had traditionally relied on men for. Our fear so far had held us back. We didn't know how to begin, and finally decided that we needed help. We invited a friend of one of our members to come to several of our meetings to teach us massage. She came as a guest, confidently and unobtrusively taught us her skills and left. We removed all our clothes except our pants, we had never seen each other's breasts, tummies, chests and nipples before – it was a revelation that there was flesh between our heads and our toes. We split into pairs and learnt to read the messages etched into the back and neck muscles. We stroked and kneaded and pummelled and loosened the knots of tension and pressure, upset and worry from each other. It was a relief not to need words. Now and again one of us got giggly. Mostly we were warm and whispered and the air smelt of body oil. I remember the relief at having taken off my clothes so that I would never have to do it for the first time again.

The glow of this first physical experience between us lasted for several months, to the extent that several of our meetings were used in this way. The second occasion sticks out in my mind. I was nervous all over again – I hung back a little in choosing a partner, and thereby I was inevitably paired with one of the other women who also felt more tentative. I was particularly close to her and she seemed also to be unsure of me. I know I felt inhibited, I also knew that I wanted to battle with it, but I was afraid to voice these feelings at the time. Suddenly my body felt ungainly and unlovable, I felt aware of my sweat and my smells, and I became even sweatier at the thought of being repulsive to my partner. She didn't reassure me either by words or touch, she clearly felt uncertain and inhibited too. We were both stuck with our fear. We massaged each other not because we wanted to but because the fear of being noticed and being singled out was even greater. Being rejected by the group for 'failing' to be free and liberated felt like a real and terrifying possibility at the time. Checked out many months later it appeared as ludicrous to me as to anyone else. Nevertheless, these feelings of terror and dis-approval to the extent that I felt as if I might be rejected, were the feelings which immobilised me and prevented me for a time from fully exploring the experiences of massage and touch in the group. The massage meetings gradually stopped, not by democratic decision-making or by feeling that we had exhausted all that we could do, at the time it felt like a natural phasing out. In retrospect and through discussion we became aware that our fears had got the better of us. Some of us were afraid of the implied sexuality, our skin, our smells, the warmth, the intimacy and the oil; it was frightening not to know where the experience was leading and how much we might be forced to reassess our responses, our feelings, our definitions. Others felt that it might lead to sexual relation-ships within the group, and the fear in that fantasy involved the group being destroyed. Yet others had without realising found it an ongoing strain to be repeatedly doing something which forced them to confront inhibitions and feelings of discomfort, and so had stopped suggesting that we continue or develop our use of massage or the learning of the skills.

Unconsciously we had made a group decision. Months later we are still in the process of reversing it.

As Socialists it was not enough for our group to be only working at an individual and group level; our politics led us to believe that we must make a public impact as well as a private one. We felt that it wasn't enough for each of us to be involved in our own trade unions or other political campaigns – the life of the group and our feminism were important determinants of this feeling. Other left-wing activity involved us in working with men and this in itself was a problem, for some of us even to the degree that we felt our available energy was being used solely to struggle against the male, competitive values of domination with our comrades. For others the values and structures that we found in the left-wing parties and trade unions mirrored our experience of the society as a whole, and left us either unable to participate, falling again into a feminine stereotype, or else the possibility of involving ourselves only by behaving like men, in order to be heard, and allowing those who were unable or unwilling, to fall by the wayside. As feminists we believe women should organise together without men, learning to find our own strengths and weaknesses, creating a new way of working and making an impact. We also felt that there were an enormous number of women who were not in waged employment, who on the whole were ignored by most of the left-wing parties, or else written off as a conservative element. We wanted to reach them as well, not only believing it to be the right course, but also because most of us know what it was like to be working at home, caring for children without a wage. Simultaneously we had another dilemma; as Socialists we were aware that ultimately women would have to struggle with as well as against men. At this point, however, we weren't ready for them, nor them for us. We decided to campaign locally for a women's centre.

Comments on 'Political therapy group'

This piece reflects the difficulties of writing openly about intimate experiences and of selecting from a long and complex process of growth, setback and retrenchment. The single dominating issue is that of the nature of change. The group is explicitly dedicated to bringing about changes: its brief is 'political', the original aim of each member is to advance the cause of socialist struggle, and at the end of the piece we are told of the decision to campaign for a women's centre as a way of making 'a public impact as well as a private one'. Perhaps it is the source of the desire to change in socialist as well as feminist politics that produces an emphasis on change as something difficult, an 'uneasy mixture of comfort and struggle'. Change is threatening and painful in itself, but frustration sets in if it is not achieved. In the early passages of the illustration it is made clear how the group protects itself against change because it is so frightening, but also how everyone feels disappointed if change is avoided and all that is offered is mutual support. This group is not willing for people to be made to feel better by simple acceptance of one another: the anti-humanist stance is adopted, that change is painful, occurring through struggle and conflict.

The emphasis on rigorous self-examination produces two contradictory trends in this group. On the one hand, it is a remarkably stable group, which has kept together over a five-year period. At points it is clear that the group processes are exhilarating: for example, the passage on the immediate response to massage ('the glow of this first physical experience') is celebratory, possibly romanticising the experience but also reflecting a genuine sense of breakthrough in an otherwise very verbally oriented group. On the other hand, often at exactly the most exhilarating points, a defensiveness sets in which seems geared towards preventing the very changes that the group is supposedly dedicated to achieving. In part, this defensiveness is visible indirectly in the author's caution over revealing disagreements: for instance, the 'grand' aim to 'exclude neither the political nor the personal' is the culmination of a passage in which the position of the group is presented as one in which political and therapeutic potential are given equal weight and are viewed as intertwined. There is no discussion of the processes by which the group arrived at this position, processes which may have been complex and uneven. The rest of the piece portrays the group as united around a common struggle for personal and political change, but also describes the protective feelings that members have for the group. It may be that this same protectiveness operates in the description of group aims, glossing over the difficulties inherent in facing personal challenges.

The author herself draws attention to two important forms that defensiveness takes. One concerns the hierarchies of acceptable feelings: 'our new list was as endless as our old one', she notes in this connection. Perhaps a movement needs to set up a new hierarchy of acceptable positions before variations and alternatives can be accepted, but the hierarchy actually used here is defensive in several respects. Hanging on to ideas of correct thinking papers over difficult feelings which may need to be confronted honestly for change to occur: for example, possessiveness or jealousy, which disappear as emotions that can be talked about. Perhaps more destructively, having a collection of acceptable and unacceptable positions ('shoulds and shouldn'ts') keeps people apart from one another, whatever their avowed group commitment. It is the detail of contradictory feelings that allows closeness and in that sense underlies real solidarity. As with the author's fears of 'being rejected by the group', the well learned internal structures creating feelings about performance, judgement and rejection have to be continually and freely struggled with as they resurface, even in the most supportive and progressive of settings. In the group, the labels and hierarchies, while they remain unchallenged, prevent progress and reinstate those feelings of having to perform or being judged that the group is ostensibly challenging.

The second form of defensiveness that the author draws attention to, though less directly, arises from her account of the gradual abandonment of massage, which at one point had liberated the group from a very stuck phase. When the massage becomes a tenable item of discussion ('many months later'), it is clear that sexual inhibitions are at the source of the anxiety. The fantasy within the group is that of 'the group being destroyed' by sexuality: all the images of sexual relations are destructive; sex is never viewed as something that can bring people together. The group is too sacred, a family that has to be protected against the ravages of sex. Somewhere, the physical closeness experienced with such joy in the massage sessions is also experienced as part of older fears and inhibitions, against intimacy and incest. This point actually relates to one of the great strengths of the group as well as its weakness: everyone wants 'the group to continue' and fears its destructiveness; it is experienced as a safe place, with much of the language used to describe it being similar to that which might be used in other circumstances to talk about a marriage or a family. The group provides experiences that are usually confined within these traditional structures; as such, it offers liberating posssibilities for renewal, a reworking of unconscious emotions, but it also carries transferred feelings of vulnerability and inhibition which, when left unanalysed, are able to reproduce in this 'political therapy group' the oppressions of the outside and internalised world.

Summary of issues from 'Therapy and struggle' illustrations

The three illustrations in this section deal more explicitly than those in the 'therapy and personal change' group with overtly political considerations: management and state power, ideology, activism. In each case, personal development is less important than group functioning, the well-being and continuing coherence of the group being particularly central in Illustrations 4 and 6. Where individuality is considered, it is in the context of the significance of personal change for successful struggle in wider spheres, for example to challenge racist ideology or to strengthen the power of the group to act effectively. This contrasts with the emphasis in the previous group of illustrations on change for the sake of the well-being and integrity of the individuals concerned. For 'Therapy and struggle', the end point of activity is political change.

Despite the difference in focus of the two groups of illustrations, several of the issues raised in the commentaries are common, and it is these commonalities that indicate crucial factors for politicised mental health practice. As was the case with the earlier illustrations, the most effective entry to the uncovering of underlying impulses and conflicts is through the analysis of defences as they are revealed in the accounts of each group. For the 'Therapy and struggle' illustrations, a common shared difficulty is in dealing with problems posed by the leadership position into which the therapist or teacher is forced. This is particularly the case with Illustrations 4 and 5; Illustration 6 circumvents the problem by having a leaderless group, although problems surrounding expertise and the use of an outsider to teach certain skills are still evident. Illustrations 4 and 5 demonstrate considerable ambivalence around leadership, the former by combining a denial that the author is a leader with expressions of guilt and uncertainty over whether the leadership demands have been adequately met; the latter by attempting to maintain the fiction of a democratic, self-motivated learning group while simultaneously adopting a directive teaching style and a lecturing attitude towards readers of the piece. Why should leadership be an issue that creates such muddled defensiveness? As in the previous illustrations, power is a difficulty for the authors, in both its negative and positive aspects. Power is identified with control, which is anathema to the self presentation of radical therapists and teachers: how can an advocate of disseminated power present her/himself as authoritarian? Similarly, for all three authors group functioning is successful when trust and mutual support are evident, but these are achievements that cannot be imposed by an outsider – groups, like individuals, have to change from within. The positive aspects of power are at least as threatening, particularly in Illustration 4. Groups are needy, dependent entities, and the leader is placed in a position at the centre of these needs: her/his power carries with it demands for help, comfort and containment of painful feelings. This is an acute and heavy responsibility that can become too strong for a group leader who is her/himself unsupported, and which, if left unanalysed, can paralyse the functioning of the group. In Illustration 4 and, to a lesser extent, Illustration 5, the therapist and teacher play down the centrality of their positions, dissipating power fictitiously around the group as a way of avoiding taking on all the needs and demands that surround them.

A strong sense of anti-intellectualism pervades all three of the illustrations in this section. This is to some extent justifiable because of the association between intellectuality and defensiveness, something demonstrated particularly clearly in Illustration 4 by the distancing devices adopted by the author, and in Illustration 5 by the commentary given alongside the description of events. The claims made by the authors that intellectualising can lead to avoidance of emotional confrontation also have their validity demonstrated in each of the groups. Nevertheless, the anti-intellectualism adopted in the descriptions (e.g. in the dismissal of anti-racist learning as 'rhetoric') sets up an opposition between the intense experiences of the members of all three groups and the thoughtful linking of those experiences with wider structural and social influences. Distinguishing between intellectual defensiveness and interpretations resulting in enhanced personal and group integrity is a difficult but important exercise.

Finally, a general point of considerable significance arises from the three illustrations in this section. All three examples are of groups, and in each case, but particularly with the long-term groups described in Illustrations 4 and 6, much of the energy of group members is devoted to the protection of their group. In Illustration 4 group members hide their relationships, pretend that the group serves the needs of their children rather than themselves, paper over disagreements and conflicts, and deny the existence of major problems. They do this to ward off what is perceived as an immense and imminent danger that the group will be destroyed by the power of the conflicts with which the Children's Home is riven. Similarly, the women's group described in Illustration 6 is presented as united throughout the piece, despite differences of opinion and orientation towards central issues; group members also experience resentments and fears that are linked to worries over exclusion from the group, and when particularly threatened the group resorts to a traditional and ideological hierarchy of acceptable positions rather than investigate the real contradictions that are present. For both these groups, members experience contradictory and painful feelings that are repressed and hence come to be experienced as hostile and dangerous. In both these examples a major threat is posed by sexuality: in the Children's Home group the actual sexual relationships between people are hidden but are viewed as threatening to the smooth functioning of the group; in the women's group the potential relations are felt to be dangerous and are shied away from to the extent that a physical exercise that has had creative effects on the group is discontinued. Uncomfortable feelings are left unanalysed, and thus retain their power to split the group, forcing greater concessions to defensiveness and making the groups less and less effective, as well as more vulnerable to powerful episodes of self-destructiveness. Exploration of this unanalysed material, these unconscious impulses that are experienced as so threatening and yet which contain so much of the energy of the group, is as essential in these more 'political' examples as in the more obviously personal instances of therapeutic practice.

In this chapter we have presented and criticised examples of therapeutic practice, and have attempted to draw out the major implications of our analyses. We have deliberately constructed the argument around a series of critiques, in part to avoid giving the impression that politically sophisticated therapeutic work is easy, being just a matter of having the correct socialist perspective. But we have also adopted this procedure for methodological reasons: we believe that the analysis of defences is the surest way to reveal the issues that underlie any apparently freely adopted position. In the next chapter we shall develop some of the points that have emerged to make a more positive statement of the form and content of a politically aware mental health practice.

5
Towards a Radical Therapeutic Practice

All the illustrations of Chapter 4 struggle in one way or another with the dominant discourse of the therapist as the 'knower', the professional expert who possesses knowledge and insight, a discourse that encourages fear, exaggerated dependency and passivity in clients and omnipotence and narcissism in workers. The authors would agree with most left-wing critics of psychiatry that this is a regrettable state of affairs. However, we believe that it is inadequate to respond by simply producing a discourse that opposes the dominant one at each point by stating that workers are not experts, should not be professionals, and so on. In the first section of this chapter, 'Challenging the Dominant Therapeutic Discourse', it is argued that a straightforward oppositional position is no substitute for analysis that separates out the positive and negative functions of the power relations inscribed by discourse. Rather, as proposed in 'The Acceptance of Power' and 'The Refusal of Power', radical practice must involve the subversion of discourse in a manner which maximises the positive possibilities for change, and this entails working with problems instead of acting as though they did not exist. This raises the issue of how to distinguish radical from conventional practices, and in 'The Purposes of Therapy' an answer is given using the concept of 'subjectification'. Finally, 'Supervision, Personal Therapy and Radical Therapists' tackles some of the practical difficulties in establishing a radical practice.

CHALLENGING THE DOMINANT THERAPEUTIC DISCOURSE

The most general lesson of Chapter 4 is that no matter how they may differ in their responses to it, each of the author's practice is unintelligible without reference to a discourse of the therapist as knowing, professional expert. Whether it is the 'individual psychotherapist' of Mr A, who endorses the role of skilled therapist, or the 'Political therapy group' of Illustration 6, which is explicitly founded on a rejection of the need for an outside expert, one may say that the experiences described are in part constructed by the dominant therapeutic discourse. This discourse, although it may seem initially to provide a unitary representation or image, contains a number of distinct elements: the therapist as the person in control, leading or directing the situation; the therapist as the person who knows, as the person possessing specialised skills; and finally as 'professional' with its multitude of associations, ranging from the assumption of an 'impersonal' relationship with clients, to implications of status and educational and class background. The combination of these elements tends to put the therapist in a position of considerable power, but it would be wrong to reject each element or the power of their combination as simply false or bad. This is in fact what the authors often do in the illustrations, causing many of their difficulties.

A good example is the question of leadership, which crops up in all four pieces involving groups. In the group situation the expectation is that the therapist is the leader and must consequently have a dominant power-laden role. The negative associations of this generalised notion have led radicals to assert the importance of leaderless groups as the means to combat traditional authoritarian structures. Yet this response avoids the issues time and again, and far from challenging the dominant ideology tends to produce a variant of it. Thus the feminist therapy group of Illustration 6 rejects the idea that groups must have leaders, but fails to confront issues of difference between the members (differing levels of skill, differing needs and personalities, etc.) which are tied up in power relationships that actually might have surfaced if there had been a leader on whom they could have centred. Because leadership problems have not been confronted, the group is unable to move away from a sometimes stultifying mutual collusion, each person being afraid of rocking the boat in case the group should sink. This problem is partially resolved by inviting an outside expert into the group to lead them in the learning of a particular skill. The specificity of the skill (massage) makes it an attractive focus for a group experiencing uncertainties around leadership because it has a discrete quality that makes it easy to keep separate from the more threatening group dynamics. With all its limitations, the massage experience was enlightening and facilitatory for the group, suggesting that the challenge to the generalised lumping together of all forms of leadership as equivalently oppressive was worthwhile.

The Children's Home group similarly wishes to be leaderless and yet quite plainly accepts and looks to the therapist's leadership in times of crisis. The problem with this is that it is a denial of the group's difficulties in relation to the hierarchical management structure within which they are situated, a denial that could easily lead to turmoil and chaos when the group most needed to function as a whole. If there is little to be gained by a group's covering up its problems over leadership, it is equally pointless for someone in a leader's role to do likewise: it is hard to see what would be lost by the racism awareness teacher making clear to the students (and to himself) that a role-play is in his view the best way of learning, and the quasi-democratic decision procedure that takes place could only undermine his position at times when, being exposed to powerful emotions, the group could well need someone around who is clear about what was happening. This danger is evident in the 'Therapy and tea-making' example, where the Centre head's denial of her position threatens to ignite an explosive situation. Fortunately the members put her under pressure to take charge and this enables some defusing of the conflict.

Similar criticisms can be made of oppositional approaches to other elements of therapeutic discourse. Thus anti-professionalism ignores the complexity of the position of helping professionals, as mentioned in Chapter 1. Equally, the view that the ideology of the expert deskills and promotes passivity in non-experts does not imply that what skills workers do have should be denied, but is rather to point out that those skills and their representation are far from being politically neutral.

What might be called 'oppositional discourse' has its roots in the negative view of power criticised in Chapter 1. The dominant discourse of the treatment relationship in mental health work is one in which the clinician imposes procedures or techniques on a 'patient', and is hence in the 'power-laden' position of expertly manipulating the other person's feelings or perceptions. Oppositional discourse therefore suggests that an alternative relationship is one in which the clinician does not have power, and the client is an equal. The trouble with this is, first, that it takes ideology at face value as a simple reflection of an oppressive reality rather than standing in a number of complex relations to it, and second, that by regarding power as a negative term to be eliminated, it leads to a search for an ideal relationship in which power does not operate. This can easily produce a pseudo-democratic, pseudo-egalitarian mode of functioning in which exactly the same forces are present as ever, except that they are unacknowledged and the words that might say so are repressed. Thus the head of a Day Centre can write Illustration 3 without mentioning her status, as if the understanding of what happened would be unaffected by that bit of information; or the leader of the Children's Home group can write as if he got involved 'by accident'.

The prevalence of oppositional discourse testifies to the negative experience of power at work: the battles against an insensitive bureaucratic hierarchy, quarrels over status between professions, statutory powers to remove people from their families, and more subtle factors such as the way a professional's word carries more weight than that of a client. Yet in order to be employed, workers have to abide by the status quo, and contribute to its maintenance, not to mention gaining from it financially and in social standing. This means that mental health work is fraught with guilt-inducing contradictions: operating at the vicious end of the system the ills of oppression and suffering are painfully obvious, reinforcing the need for political change, but the worker is inevitably part of that system, reaping its benefits and seemingly unable qua worker to alter its power structure. It is small wonder, then, that the traditional power balance is easily 'rejected' at the same time as being surreptitiously exploited, and that a discourse is produced that obscures and denies the power relations actually obtaining. Unfortunately this deletion of reality disguises contradictions as much as the discourse to which it opposes itself, resulting in a failure to explore properly the constituent elements of therapeutic relationships, particularly the manner in which the positive aspects of power can aid change. Rather than take the negative *experience* of power as a mirror reflection of its true operation, it is important to take it as *information* about the way power relations operate – information that must be analysed and integrated with other elements of therapy and practice, in the same way as negative feelings about a client can be used to help understand something going on in the relationship between client and therapist rather than as a reflection of the client's negative qualities.

The development of an effective political practice therefore requires a recognition and a working with the relationships between worker, work setting and client. As both socialists and therapists, we believe it is vital to acknowledge the impossibility of escape from power relations, and so the problem is not how to reject them but how to take up a viable position in relation to them. There are two ways in which the position taken by the therapist with respect to power relations can challenge the dominant therapeutic discourse: the *acceptance of power*, facilitating the opening up of experiences and feelings to analysis and hence to the making of new connections between psychological distress and social reality; and the *refusal of power* in order to leave the client better able to integrate these connections and maintain them independently of the therapist. We shall outline both these positions with reference to the illustrations of Chapter 4.

THE ACCEPTANCE OF POWER

Therapy involves the taking of considerable risks by the client, not simply in entrusting her/himself to the scrutiny of another human being, but also by letting go of established behaviour and relationship patterns, raising the prospect of being left confused and vulnerable. It is certainly the case that therapists may exploit this circumstance oppressively, but it is also possible to see how they might provide the sense of containment which allows change to occur. For example, in Illustration 1 ('Individual psychotherapy') the therapist initially permits the client to overstep the boundaries of the session by extending its time. On the face of it this might appear to be a way in which the client is controlling what is going on and hence a sign of his own powerfulness. However, the therapist picks up the falseness of this in his own unease over what is happening and, through a very direct interpretation, reimposes a boundary on the client and exerts his role as the person who decides when the sessions will start and end. This has a paradoxical effect on the client: rather than subdue him or provoke a contest, it frees him to talk about the 'mess in him' in a way he has never before been able to broach, making new connections between his behaviour and his hidden inner world. Apparently, the imposition of time boundaries by the therapist has been experienced by the client as the provision of a safe container for what are chaotic and frightening feelings. This allows him to begin to use the sessions creatively to explore his dilemmas and difficulties in direct contact with the therapist, rather than avoiding them or spilling his feelings out in a self-destructive and uncontrolled way. The client comes to be more in control, more able to act on his own life as a direct consequence of the therapist's putting into words a feeling that was previously unconscious, thereby enabling it to become part of the client's conscious knowledge and understanding of himself. Such a clear imposition of caring boundaries may have been beneficial in some of the other illustrations, for instance to enable the group members in Illustration 3 to confront the conflicts in the group without them being terrifying, or to offset the most destructive aspects of the outbursts described at the end of Illustration 4 – another example, by the way, of a situation in which time boundaries were important.

The acceptance of power does not just involve the imposition of boundaries. In a few of the illustrations, progress is made by the uncovering of conflicts, either within individuals (e.g. Illustration 6, with the threat posed by physical contact) or in groups. There can be little doubt, for instance, about the directing role taken by the teacher in Illustration 5 ('Racial awareness training') yet this directiveness creates the circumstances under which conflicts cannot be ignored, but are expressed in the full awareness of their social determination. More subtly, the group leader in Illustration 4 makes use of his special position (not having to disclose his own feelings, licence to comment on the actions of others, ability to direct the drift of the session) to challenge the group's interpretation of events. In this example the therapist addresses at different times both the group's internal dynamics and the group's perception of its relation to the external world. Thus, in the incident with Alice's 'mothering' role (p. 108), the position of the therapist is used to uncover a set of unconscious assumptions which the group is papering over but which are having a significant impact on it, while in the 'union' episode (p. 110) the therapist challenges the group to confront issues that turn out to be directly related to their social position as low-level helping professionals caught in an industrial conflict. Linked to this is the provision of interpretations, again exploiting the special position of the therapist as licensed commentator, but also making use of the emotional charge of the relationship between therapist and client. The effective aspects of the therapist's 'making interpretations' is not simply the naming of feelings, but is a more complex process linked with the therapist's role of making the unconscious conscious. Thus the 'bringing in the inspectors' interpretation of Illustration 1 (p. 84) obviously relies on the therapist being in the position to make threatening comments, but also gains therapeutic efficacy through following on from the changed nature of the relationship between therapist and client that has arisen from the provision of clearer boundaries. The interpretation in Illustration 4 concerning Alice's mothering has similar determinants, and is in striking contrast to the failure of the therapist to interpret the later conflict over Andy (p. 111), a failure that may be linked to the therapist's abrogation of his position of leadership. It is thus at the point where power is denied that the therapist is least effective, where it is accepted that progress occurs.

THE REFUSAL OF POWER

The refusal of power is important for several reasons. First, in any therapeutic work the therapist needs to be available to the emotional material that is presented. As this is frequently disturbing and frightening, there is a tendency in all of us to 'not hear it' or avoid dealing with or responding to it. To allow ourselves to experience and understand these feelings that are being offered by the client, both consciously and unconsciously, it is necessary first of all to have a strong sense of personal boundaries, so that there is no confusion between the patient's feelings and those of the therapist and the therapist is not in danger of being overwhelmed. It is then necessary for the therapist to be able to cope with uncertainty and lack of understanding: however sympathetic, no one is able immediately to grasp the complexities of someone else's inner world – it is a slow, arduous process of picking up feelings, making links, trying them out, reflecting them back, and readjusting 'knowledge' and assumptions. In other words, to be able to understand another person in such a way as to be able usefully and creatively to make the therapeutic interventions, one needs to be able to tolerate getting things wrong, changing one's opinion, using one's feelings in different ways, as well as simply not knowing. It is therefore crucial that the therapist does not slot into the fantasy of the clinician's role, that s/he is all-knowing and all-understanding, and is therefore able expertly to manipulate other people's feelings or personalities and take decisions for them or give them advice. This refusal of power can be particularly hard when the patient is likely to be transferring feelings on to the therapist of being a very needy child in search of total care (understanding) and nurturance (the removal of pain). A therapist who falls into the trap of taking care of someone in this way may have a detrimental effect on the patient, who then becomes less likely to discover new connections between the conscious and the unconscious and therefore even less likely to remould the split between her/himself and the social forces that contributed to her/his suffering in the first place.

Illustration 2, 'Therapy in social work', provides us with an example of a worker who has been able to tolerate a situation in which very distressing and intense feelings are expressed in the session. Not only that, but many of them are directed at the worker as if they are personally linked up with her. By offering this kind of space and encouraging expression of feelings, the worker allows the children an opportunity to discover that their rage, terror and chaos are tolerable; they begin to learn that it may be possible to heal some of the splits that have already been internalised; they may find out that someone else can understand what they feel and not admonish them for their 'bad', messy side. In other words, instead of reinforcing a split between good and bad parts of the world and of themselves, the worker helps the children explore good and bad as indissoluble parts of everything. This should offer the children a better chance of being able to acknowledge the pain of their experience as well as the positives, instead of repressing whole areas of their lives, which ultimately would leave them with less control over their own experience, past and present, and therefore over their futures, too.

The worker's refusal of power in this example is even more critical than in others, because of her own active and very central role in removing the children from their mother, placing them with another family and subsequently maintaining this situation rather than letting them return home. Because of this the children's anger towards the worker was in part really meant for her, for what she had done to them, as well as projected anger towards their own mother for her neglect and for letting them go (rejecting them). Therefore being able to tolerate this anger had an additional possible effect, that of legitimating it and its expression, helping the children learn that it is possible to do so and not necessarily be punished or rejected as a result.

Accepting this anger as legitimate might be particularly difficult, because the anger is focused on the very point where the main contradictions of a social worker's role lie (this is particularly true for radical workers). The problematic area is their statutory powers to intrude into personal lives and family composition. The guilt felt about this kind of power often leads the worker to experience the client's anger as a deeply personal threat, which in turn leads to defensive manoeuvres designed to keep the anger under cover, giving the client the sense that the feelings are unacceptable, that they are ugly and too dangerous to be allowed out. In the long term these kinds of processes have a subtle but sinister effect of making anger even harder to express; therefore in a situation like this one there is a subversive element of encouraging this expression and making it clear that the worker recognises this response as legitimate. Additionally, she has resisted the attraction at this point of taking on the role of therapist-as-rescuer. The destructive, chaotic and hurt feelings that the children have are frequently very uncomfortable. It is tempting as rescuer to comfort, blunt, 'take-away' discomfort and pain, and then to be loved as the perfect mother. To refuse this scenario, and instead to encourage expression of these feelings, even while not understanding how they relate or fit into what has happened, leaves the children as whole people who can respond to the world without it being wrong or bad to have feelings. They have the chance, therefore, to emerge with a greater sense of their own identity intact, in spite of their extremely vulnerable predicament.

Illustration 4 also gives us an example of the worker refusing the power of 'knowing what ought to be talked about' or 'knowing what the real issues are'. Initially, he was offering the staff group advice and professional support for working with the children. This format altered after a year, becoming a group in which the staff focused on their own feelings, their relationships with each other, and their political dilemmas. This meant that the staff were eventually able to make some links, not only between their professional and personal lives, but also with their political activity in a wider context. These links enabled them to explore the ways in which their anger and splitting were creating havoc in their relationships with each other, immobilising them with distress and confusion when they were faced with the political choices of trade union activity. Resolving some of these freed them to explore the links with power and politics in a wider context. This exemplifies how the space offered by the therapist and the resultant interpretations opened up the possibility of following through their explorations on to more frightening, unknown ground which ultimately has more subversive potential. If the therapist had provided a space but had limited the context to 'professional support', this fuller therapeutic intervention could not have taken place. This is in direct contradiction to a commonly held left-wing view, that talking about feelings and personal relationships is self-indulgent and individualistic. When, as in this context, these kinds of discussions help people to act, they add to the subversive power of therapy.

Lastly, having described various ways in which therapists must refuse the power of 'knowing what is best for someone else', it is important to note another aspect to the refusal of power. This is the encouragement of independence in the client, leaving her/him with the ability to integrate new connections into their lives without the therapist. This should be a feature of the entire process, not just the ending of therapy, as Illustration 4 shows. Here the author describes how he felt unable to continue to lead the group after a while, because he was 'over-identified' with the members and their interrelationships and therefore unable to intervene as usefully as he would have liked. In spite of this problem, however, he was obviously not so over-involved as to fail to recognise what was occurring. In addition, his leadership of the group had not been of such a kind as to undermine seriously the group's ability to continue without him. They were therefore able to allow him to leave, and subsequently they could decide as a group that they wanted to continue the work with someone else. A therapist who had domineered the group could have precipitated immobilising anger and fragmentation by leaving the group. The group would have been more likely to experience the loss as totally debilitating, and therefore the potential for growth – professional, personal and political – would have been ultimately in the hands of the therapist and not the group.

THE PURPOSES OF THERAPY

Many political critiques of psychotherapy have adopted the position that therapy is by nature bourgeois or reactionary, because it is concerned with individuals rather than social collectives, and because of what is seen to be the ideological domination of the client by the therapist, or even because it ameliorates pain rather than allowing it to fester, eventually to break out as a revolutionary running sore. From this position the only legitimate mode of political struggle is in direct political action, aimed at the state or its institutional manifestations. Although we do not wish to devalue the centrality of direct action, we do not accept that it is the only level at which political struggle can take place. Psychological therapies can contain progressive as well as conformist possibilities because they operate at the interface of social and personal concerns, and their impact is therefore potentially instructive for socialist ideas and practice.

Attacks on bourgeois therapeutic practice that are less dismissive have largely focused on elements such as the emphasis on individual rather than group treatment, the reactive rather than preventive organisation of services, and their localisation in the hospital rather than the community. It is important to consider these points, and the central issue of 'community care' is taken up in Chapter 6. However, to make them the basis of an assault on dominant practices is to neglect the arena in which power relations make themselves felt during therapy, the interaction between therapist and client. As argued in Chapter 2, it is through the direct contact with her/his caretakers that the organisational principles of society become internalised. Similarly, it is in the immediate encounter between client and therapist that power relations are replayed and re-experienced, either confirming their original structure or being demolished and born anew. Therapy is often thought of as rarified and separate, as though different processes take place from those in other relationships; it is rather a situation where the variables are cut down to a minimum, making processes such as the reproduction of power relations and the transference of feelings and responses from early life more visible and therefore more analysable.

It can be seen, then, that traditional left-wing critiques of therapy ignore the complexities of people's internal states and relationships with others. Paradoxically, this has gone hand in hand with a fascination with madness that both denies the prevalence of psychotic processes in everyday life and pays no attention to the more ordinary distress that is the bread and butter of mental health practice: depression, anxiety and lack

of self-confidence may not have the glamour that has somehow become associated with the concept of madness, but may
have more to tell us politically. The failings of these critiques
can be traced theoretically to their negative, external conception of power and a correlative view of ideology as a set of false
ideas. This results in mental health services being regarded as
the institutional exercise of social control by a negative
external force (the state) and its practice as either the
tranquillising into silence of people who refuse to conform, or
the imposition of a distorted view of society on an oppressed,
passive recipient. The specifics of therapeutic skills and
processes are untheorised, as if they are of no interest or
neutral, like a machine over which the only dispute is
ownership. However, in Chapter 4 examples of practice in a
variety of settings uncovered issues that did not seem to
depend on any particular arrangement of services for their
presence. These arise from the *internal* connections between
discourse and power, ideology and emotion. It is the existence
of these connections that makes the substitution of an oppositional discourse for the dominant discourse so inadequate. To
develop an alternative, closer consideration is needed of the
point of exposure of client to therapist, for it is there that
politics is experienced in its most tangible form. We shall do
this by looking in greater depth at the factors determining the
therapist's position in relation to power.

What we have called the acceptance and refusal of power
are linked to questions of general political relevance that are
especially sharply defined in mental health practice. Examination of these will enable a more precise definition of a
radical therapeutic practice. Most important are the related
issues of the setting within which change can take place and
the relationship that can facilitate it. The nature of change is
too complicated a question to be addressed here in detail but
two points are of particular importance: that the boundaries of
the client/worker relationship need to be clearly defined, and
that interventions seem most effective when they take into
account that relationship, and can be noticeably ineffectual if
they do not. Thus the time, length and setting of meetings
between client and worker are not incidental details to be
arranged according to convenience, but provide the basic

structure within which work takes place. Any variation is likely to have powerful effects on the unconscious phantasy of the client, and correspondingly attempts to vary boundaries by the client, even if accepted by the worker for practical reasons, need to be carefully considered for their meaning. This is evident in Illustration 1, where the effects of the re-imposition of boundaries is dramatic, but it is equally true, if less obviously, in the other illustrations. In Illustration 6, for example, the massage teacher is invited to help the group overcome its inhibitions about physical contact. The appearance that the teacher 'confidently and unobtrusively taught us her skills' and then leaves the group members better able to explore together is undermined by the author's admission that she and her partner 'massaged each other not because [they] wanted to, but because the fear of being noticed and singled out was even greater'. In this group unspoken pressures, norms of behaviour and feeling, a sense of what is and is not acceptable, impede the members' ability to voice their anxieties, and in fact they go ahead with the massage sessions despite the welter of conscious feelings of ambivalence, fear, repulsion and desire that are aroused. The impetus cannot be maintained indefinitely and the meetings fade away, the unresolved feelings stunting the further development of the group. However, one can surmise that it is not just the strength of the conscious feelings that leads to resistance to continuation: the implicit sexual intimacy of the massage sessions inevitably generates anxieties and stimulates phantasies whose strength is indicated by the group's conscious feelings, but are themselves more deeply rooted and inaccessible. It is only when the group's boundaries are re-established by the exit of the massage teacher and its individual members' physical and psychological boundaries are no longer directly threatened that the group can begin to re-establish a space for growth.

Boundaries are not just established by the structure of the therapeutic encounter, but are constantly in question during it, in the interaction between client and therapist. Each utterance, whatever else it may say, says something about the boundary between the two, and much of what happens can be construed as an attempt to test out or understand the meaning of the definition of their relationship. Illustration 3, for example, describes an incident sparked off by a disturbing intrusion that crosses agreed boundaries – the member of one group going into the kitchen when she is not supposed to – and in relation to the head of the centre can be seen as a testing of her ability to maintain boundaries, and of her relationship to the clients. The Centre's functioning is threatened when this is unclear. This example is interesting because it emphasises the importance of boundaries, whether the situation is one in which the therapist *does* things with clients or only talks to them. This implies that boundaries are significant in the understanding not just of 'therapeutic' situations but in all human activities and relationships. This might be obvious in the case of friends and lovers, but may be less so in political activity where the understandable stress on doing things can lead to a denial of aspects of group functioning that may be seriously impeding its ability to fulfil its task. An example might be meetings that always start and end late, a phenomenon often rationalised as mere 'informality'. It could, however, mean many things – an unconscious agreement to try to exclude certain members, anxiety about the difficulty of the task, and so on. Whatever the meaning, distortions or disturbances of boundaries are worthy of attention.

Change, of course, does not take place as a product of clear boundaries, however helpful these might be. In therapy it comes out partly through clarifying thoughts and feelings, but mostly through the gradual increase in awareness of factors previously outside of consciousness. The therapist's main tool in this process is the use of words to make interpretations, a use quite different from the communication of information or making conversation. Interpretations are not effective if they come out of the blue; they must refer to the client's state as expressed in the therapeutic situation, and this will often involve 'transference interpretations' – that is, interpretations that refer to the client's feelings about the therapist. Thus in Illustration 1 the therapist's interpretation of the client's extending the session is not just an imposition of boundaries but links the client's behaviour with his feelings about the therapist. A fuller interpretation still might relate these feelings to past experiences with parents. The therapist or worker's words have a double aspect: they do not just make connections in the client's experience but also link the therapist to certain discourses which might in turn affect the relationship. This is so even in this illustration, where the therapist is being as 'neutral' as possible – for example, this commenting on the length of sessions links him to a 'professional' discourse within which contractual arrangements are made and where the power relations between profession and clients are routinely obscured by the apparently egalitarian purchase of services. This has some analogy with the employer/employee relationship referred to by the client later in the session. In other illustrations this involves a more clear-cut decision on the part of the author: the leader of the Children's Home group decides to link himself with a left-wing political discourse, the teacher links himself to the attempt to create a non-racist discourse, the women's self-help group debates its relationship to the political discourse that stresses action and campaigns.

As well as linking her/himself to various discourses, the therapist may do the same to the client, deliberately or otherwise, and this raises the question of whether to set out with the intention of doing this or not. There is a spectrum that runs from the attempt at complete neutrality of the psychoanalyst at one end and the sloganising propaganda campaign at the other. We have already argued that the therapist's refusal of power means the acceptance of uncertainty, the refusal to adopt a position of knowledge and control, but this does not necessarily exclude the making of interpretations that point out the client's position in ideology or power relations. To what extent a radical therapeutic practice should include reference to ideology is, we believe, a central and constant dilemma to which there can be no single answer – it needs to be thought about in each case. For the moment, though, it is worth pointing out that it is a dilemma that should perhaps be taken rather more seriously in more straightforward political activity: for wherever there is a battle for change there must be a change in awareness or ideas as well as practice; and as we have been at pains to stress, ideas are not just linked through discourse to power relations of diverse kinds, but also to unconscious and conscious feelings that need to be registered in order for change to come about. This is *not* to say that large-scale political change involves some kind of mass therapy, but to reiterate that the internal sources of resistance to change should not be ignored or underestimated.

Concentration on therapeutic processes allows a more precise approach to the question of how radical practice might differ from bourgeois practices. One way of doing this is to develop a distinctive set of aims for radical therapy: the extent to which particular therapeutic procedures might be called 'progressive' can then be calibrated by assessing the extent to which they make fulfilment of these aims more likely. Although its rhetoric employs the language of 'treatment', non-psychoanalytic bourgeois therapies are primarily concerned with *management* at the individual level by helping people control their symptons or feel better about themselves without changing too much; at the social level by contributing to the mental health policies directed at the smooth running of the social order. This is clear in ordinary medical practice, for example in the use of tranquillisers or antidepressants to enable women to cope with the stresses of domestic labour, or in the provision of sick notes to allow a worker to rest enough to be able to return to the stresses of the workplace. Psychiatry is similarly dominated by the tendency to objectify people – to treat them and their suffering as objects – the equivalent of the medical 'liver in ward 14' approach: the aims are symptom-control, stabilisation.

The liberal, humanistic response to the extremes of psychiatric objectification is to oppose it by focusing on the subjective account that the individual gives of her/his experiences, thus coming to understand and treat her/him as a fully human being whose communications are meaningful and worthy of respect. We support this as far as it goes, but believe it has limitations that prevent it from ever providing the full basis for a radical approach to therapy. Most importantly, this 'humanistic' perspective assumes the validity of phenomenological reports: that is, it holds to a view of individuality that makes a person's consciousness the final arbiter of their motivations or responses. Treating people seriously is

central to good therapeutic practice, but prioritising consciousness makes the essentialist error of considering them as
unique and particular 'selves' that exist outside of sociality
and which have access to all aspects of internal functioning.
We dispute both these claims and believe that in the end they
result in a conformist therapeutic procedure that can do no
more than accept what a person has to say about her/himself
and hope that this acceptance will make the person feel better.
Although this 'client-centred' approach deals more directly
with emotions and can lead to some personal growth, it does
not address the psychological or political structures within
which experience is taking place, and so cannot alter the
client's basic position within those structures. It therefore
amounts to little more than a 'softer' form of objectification
that doesn't change anything but makes things more bearable
in the nicest possible way.

It is in opposition to the hard and soft management
orientations of psychiatry that Chapter 3 adopted a 'subversive' outlook on therapy as on politics, 'not just subversion of
here-and-now social reality, but subversion of the past as it is
being lived out in the here and now' (p. 78). Just as our
analysis of psychological distress emphasises the links between individual experience and social discourse, so therapy
can operate at nodal points in the social fabric, where
ideological constructions and personal encounters intertwine.
A radical therapeutic practice must aim not at maintaining or
repairing current modes of personal and social organisation,
but at subverting them by challenging the assumptions and
unconscious structures that dominate psychological functioning, and demonstrating their links with large-scale political
processes. These links must not be made intellectually,
through argument and exposition, but experientially, so that
the lived reality of the individual's existence is altered. This is
a great deal to demand of therapy, geared as it is to the
treatment of individuals, families or groups suffering psychological pain. It is difficult to see how a general concept like
'subversion' can provide an orienting framework for the
specifics of therapeutic practice. How is one to know if a
particular intervention is subversive or not? What is it about
an intervention that makes it more or less subversive than

another? In contrast to the objectifying tendencies of psychiatry or humanistic psychotherapy, we wish to introduce the notion of radical therapeutic practice as 'subjectifying', the degrees of 'subjectification' of people's experience being a measure of subversiveness. The concept of subjectification can also be used to highlight the political dilemmas facing would-be radical therapists, as we explain below.

Subjectification as a goal is distinct from the humanistic approach because it prioritises subjectivity while opposing the idea that the self is free and undetermined. Throughout this book we have stressed the ways in which people are *subject* to forces that construct their selves. These forces are of two kinds. First, psychoanalysis reveals that people are subject to the unconscious: that is, their behaviour, thoughts and feelings are directed by the forces of the unconscious, by desires, impulses or ideas that are inaccessible to conscious control. Second, socialist theory reveals that people are subject to social forces – economic, political, ideological – which are more powerful and extensive than them and which have systematic effects on behaviour and consciousness. In both cases the connections between conscious experience and the forces that operate upon it are routinely obscured, the difficulty in perceiving as well as controlling them enhancing their power. Additionally, as argued in Chapters 1–3, these two sets of forces are linked: the unconscious is structured around the dimensions prescribed by sociality, while the social order depends for its maintenance on the way dominant power relations (e.g. patriarchal and capitalist ones) are internalised by the individual psyche and replicated in a wide range of microsocial encounters. To the extent that these connections and the determining forces that lie behind them are uncovered and resisted, a (politically) subversive change is taking place. One arena in which such changes can take place is that of psychological therapy: through some forms of therapy people can be brought to experience themselves as 'subject' in both the ways described above, to the unconscious and to the forces of the social world. 'Subjectification' thus refers to a dual function of radical therapy: to reveal to the individual the way in which s/he is subject to unconscious forces and to pursue the analysis of these forces until their social determinants are also uncovered. Through unconscious subjectification, social subjectification may also arise, although the two are not identical.

It is in its stress on the possibility of social subjectification that our position differs from that of conventional psychoanalysis. Clearly, there are commonalities: both approaches show concern for the alleviation of distress, focus on individual experience and tend to take place over a long period – years rather than months. Both emphasise the importance of boundaries and the use of interpretation, the toleration of uncertainty, the slow process of internal change with its painstaking exploration, confirmation, dismantling and rebuilding of psychic structures, the need to work with the transference and relate it to early experience. However, we believe that the traditional psychoanalytic concept of the therapist's 'neutrality' belies the internal significance of ideology and power relations, leading to an objectification of social relations and a false separation of subjectivity from the discourses in which it is embedded. This results in an unnecessary political conformism and restriction of the boundaries of the therapeutic situation and the interpretations that may be made. We are not suggesting that therapists should start spouting political dogma, but that the definition of the aims of therapy may be extended to include social subjectification. The conventional objection to this is that it would inhibit regression and the exploration of the deepest layers of the client's unconscious. It is not clear to us why this should be so: as we have stated, it is naive to assume that it is possible to escape from power relations, so no matter how the therapist defines boundaries, a position in relation to them is being adopted, however inexplicit. It must be acknowledged, though, that explicitly introducing the social into therapy will inevitably produce difficult dilemmas for the therapist, because the relation between social and unconscious subjectification is so complex; but we would insist on it because it is this order of complexity that the politics of mental health must grapple with.

A misconceived criticism often levelled at psychoanalysis is that it endorses the intellect over the emotions. In fact, interpretations only acquire meaning through their emotional truth rather than intellectual credibility: insight includes both feeling and understanding. Furthermore, subjectification will be impossible if experienced as part of a context of personal oppression or lack of contact between client and therapist. Our criticism of psychoanalysis is in a way the opposite: that it regards exploration of the social as an intellectual matter and therefore excludes it from consideration. This *is* a version of the split between intellectual insight and emotional experience, and one to be rejected in all its forms.

We have suggested that many traditional therapeutic relationships are alienating, encouraging the individual to split off her/his suffering and hand it over to an expert for diagnosis and treatment. These parts of people are treated as not-them, subjected to technological control (drugs, ECT) or environmental manipulation (behaviour modification). Other forms of therapy like encounter groups and many family therapies also involve an alienating process because they reinforce the barriers between consciousness and unconscious or social forces, increasing the powerlessness of the individual while seemingly modifying it. Subjectification in our sense directly opposes this alienation by reconnecting split-off parts of the psyche, revealing their inner determinants and the links between them and the social world. Alienation perpetuates dominant modes of social organisation by obscuring the connections between the internal and external world. Subjectification combats this by both severing destructive links and forging new ones. It is subversive because it points the finger at the meaning of distress, declaring the possibility of new ways of being. The split between 'intellect' and 'affect' is in this light a psychological and social defence, preventing hidden feelings from being linked to perceptions that threaten the superficial truths of common sense.

Subjectification is subversive because it places individuals in greater control, makes them more integrated, better able to act. It is not a process that is confined to therapy; it is part of all political practice. Therapy is nevertheless an important arena for subjectification because within it the forces that construct the personality can be explored and renegotiated in a way that allows the 'subject' more control. *Radical* therapeutic practice is distinguished by the importance it assigns to the reworking of the power relations structured into the therapeutic encounter itself.

SUPERVISION, PERSONAL THERAPY AND RADICAL THERAPISTS

We have argued that the politics of mental health is located as much at the point of contact between client and therapist as in the organisation of services. Being a political mental health worker is therefore not simply a matter of following some general political lines or rules derived from a critique of institutional structures and practices, but involves openness to political issues as they arise in the process of therapy in a way that may be unpredictable and specific to each client. This is a heavy demand, made all the more difficult to meet by the likelihood that work takes place within organisations unsympathetic to radical politics. In this section we consider some factors that can affect the ability of therapists to work in the way we have proposed.

It is a truism that psychotherapists and helping professionals choose their line of work according to their own psychopathology: that is, that work in some way fulfils important unconscious personal needs. In itself, the idea that the desire to help others has motivations other than pure altruism is uninformative and uncontentious and is easily used to dismiss the value of the work carried out. To be a useful observation, the nature of these needs must be identified: are there motives for therapeutic work that systematically recur in socialists drawn to this field of activity? If so, how can they be understood and turned to best account? For example, therapeutic activity is sometimes motivated by a rather general social concern, or guilt at being better off and more privileged than other people – the do-gooder syndrome. It may also arise out of a sense of incapacity when faced with the enormity of injustice in the world: at least through therapy one may be capable of easing the distress of a few individuals. In addition, a dominant discourse of therapy includes some attractively dramatic elements (e.g. Mary Barnes's description of her 'journey through madness' in Barnes and Berke, 1971 or Axline's 1964 description of her breakthrough with 'Dibs'). In a world where the possibilities of real-life drama are small, therapy can appear appealingly 'heavy', an appeal which links with common rescue fantasies to produce some of the flavour of the descriptions of Illustration 2. There is also no escaping unconscious narcissistic or sadistic motivation; for example, one might unconsciously deny or triumph over one's own neediness or anxieties, projecting them into others, in which case 'therapy' may well consist of controlling threatening aspects of oneself, rather than having much to do with the client. All therapists will have all kinds of motives which may vary from moment to moment – one minute one may be genuinely helping someone, the next trying to prove what a good therapist one is – and this will be true no matter how radical or consciously well-meaning one may be. Thus the important issue is not to judge each other's motives, but to analyse them so that their influence over practice can be understood and controlled. This is particularly so with two factors that appear widespread in the illustrations of Chapter 4, and which will inevitably be present in some measure in much radical mental health practice: identification, and the fear of losing control.

Socialists might understandably identify with politically like-minded or oppressed clients. This may be a way in which predominantly middle-class workers can become vicariously proletarian, but can also operate at a less self-serving level. For example, in Illustration 2 the social worker feels for the children not just as objects of her rescue fantasies, but also as subjects in distress: that is, she takes on their suffering almost to the extent of being swamped by it, she feels their feelings from the inside. This adds a passion to her work, but also places obstacles in the way of her search for a clear direction for her activity. In Illustration 4, the worker identifies with the Children's Home group in a variety of ways. For instance, he aligns himself explicitly with their trade union struggle, giving a clear message of support and orienting all his interpretations to increasing their capacity for opposition to management. When Andy is sent to prison, the worker clearly is affected by the events and intensifies his caring activities in the group accordingly. More subtly, from the start of the 'sensitivity' group he is drawn into the group's own difficulties over leadership because they mesh with his own confusions over the correct attitude to take towards the conventional image of the 'powerful therapist'; this results in the worker sharing the group's problem and being unable to help them deal with it. These examples point to the positive and negative consequences of identification with one's clients: identification adds a passion and concern to one's work which may mobilise a therapist to give of her/his best, but it runs the risk of resulting in an absorption into the confusions of the client which makes it impossible to help in the process of subjectification. This negative consequence is most likely to occur when identification is not recognised, but governs the therapeutic process invisibly.

The second general factor in some ways is linked to the issue of identification with clients. Everybody holds within themselves a potential for disintegration: this is a necessary consequence of the formation of the individual through a process of splitting and re-integration of mental elements. Because of this underlying potential for disintegration, certain activities or ideas will be experienced as frightening, breakdown into a state of chaotic lack of structure being the feared consequence. Avoidance of such breakdown can be a powerful motivation for a variety of activities, including therapeutic ones. This can be seen operating at the individual and group levels. Thus in Illustration 3 the behaviour of the members of the Day Centre and of the group leader can be understood as being geared towards staving off the collapse of interpersonal relationships that appears to threaten the Centre, a collapse which is feared as potentially engulfing, destroying precarious boundaries and the safety of orderly functioning. This may be the reason why the group leader does not make the clients confront the conflicts that arise, instead acceding in their self-protective displacements. In Illustration 2, at the point where the girls are most uncontrolled, the therapist imposes her own structure on the sessions, preventing the children exploding all over her, a possibility made all the more threatening by her own identification with them. In Illustration 6, the women's group exists in the unspoken awareness that it could be destroyed by the force of the contradictions present within it and by the demands arising from hidden needs and desires, particularly over sexuality. The unacknowledged way in which this awareness operates results in the group process shifting to one of appeasement rather than critical exploration.

In more general terms the actual choice to become a therapist can itself be influenced by the fear of psychosis, of the possible breakdown of one's own fragile integrity. Being a therapist is a contradictory phenomenon. On the one hand, it places one in direct exposure to human pain, thus increasing the chance of personal breakdown through the threat to one's own psychological defences. On the other hand, it allows one to regain control by appeasing the other's pain, at the same time allowing one to experience a vicarious sense of nurturance through the nurturing of others. In a sense, what goes on may be comparable to the 'compulsion to repeat' which Freud observed in his neurotic patients: that is, the seemingly inexplicable way in which people repeatedly place themselves in disturbing situations. For therapists, the compulsion to repeat may have largely satisfactory results: in a context in which, because of the power relations operating, one can control another's expressions of disturbance, one can repeatedly be confirmed in the fiction that one's own integrity is secure. The problem, however, is that the price that has to be paid for this confirmation may be the inhibition of precisely those feelings, demands and disturbances that are at the centre of the client's distress. Other social and political factors, no doubt, will also have played an important role in the therapist's choice of career. It has a respectability about it, as well as intellectual, academic and verbal requirements that render the profession and the training programme virtually solely middle class. In addition, the nurturing aspects of therapy make it an easier choice for educated middle-class women, in that it provides them with a career and therefore the possibility of financial independence without seriously challenging the dominant discourse of femininity – that is what women are 'naturally' good at.

Recognition of the necessity for conscious awareness of the therapist's motivations and the way they influence the process

of therapy places additional burdens on mental health workers. It is not sufficient to be evaluating the subjectificatory
potential of every intervention; it is also important to remain
separate but engaged and attentive, that is, to maintain a
helpful distance from the client, which nevertheless involves
genuine empathy, and to be aware of the operation of one's
own defences in tolerating or failing to tolerate the threat of
breakdown. Traditionally psychotherapists have had their
own professional structures to help them cope with the
complexities of therapeutic work that have operated during
their training period and sometimes beyond. The most important of these are intensive supervision of their 'cases', and a
personal therapy undergone by the trainee therapist her/
himself. There are problems with these structures for radical
therapists: training therapy sometimes amounts to a requirement for uncritical initiation into traditional ways of thinking,
with political commitment liable to be interpreted as psychopathology; inappropriate supervision can similarly prevent
the construction of new ways of working, not least through the
replication of hierarchical relationships. Nevertheless, both
supervision and personal therapy are invaluable in allowing
workers to approach their encounters with clients creatively
and helpfully. Supervision, in the sense of a setting in which
therapeutic work can be intensively discussed and explored, is
crucial for all mental health workers at all stages of their
careers. Good supervision at least allows one to explore new
techniques and provides a forum for overcoming 'stuckness'.
More importantly it enables analysis of 'counter-transference'
to occur: that is, the important separation of what feelings
are arising from the client and what has been brought to the
work by the therapist her/himself. In this way the exposure to
a critical but supportive other person can help in differentiat-
ing the various components of the complex process of therapy,
in the provision of helpful boundaries and in the maintenance
of realistic positions.

We are aware that this is an idealised view of many people's
actual experience: supervision can be a demoralising experience, and the traditional one-to-one supervision in which an
'expert' advises a less experienced worker may simply reinforce the stultifying and oppressive structures which radicals

are committed to opposing. This is not, however, a reason to reject supervision altogether: it is essential to consider whether there are alternative ways in which supervision can be organised, as this would be the only way in which workers could provide themselves with a chance of maintaining and developing a critical practice; for example, through peer supervision, or supervision in a group of workers all committed to a radical perspective. These kinds of groups demand a level of openness and trust (as well as sufficient political agreement) that may be elusive in many work situations. This means that they will often need to be organised outside the workplace: our comments on the illustrations of Chapter 4 arose from just such a supervisory experience. There is no doubt that it is impossible to sustain a critical practice alone, any more than one could be an active trade unionist without a trade union.

The traditional psychoanalytic opinion that a personal 'training analysis' is a vital prerequisite for becoming a therapist extends the supervision argument still further. At the least, personal therapy is valuable in exposing workers to the receiving end of a procedure which they will shortly be imposing on other people, so usefully challenging the power relations that usually prevail for any individual therapist. Additionally, this may enable a worker to perceive, through emotional experience, differences between interventions that are primarily helpful and liberating, and those that are primarily blunting or oppressive. Personal therapy extends the supervisory function of clarifying boundaries and counter-transferences by helping workers perceive their own needs and desires in a broader context than that of their interactions with clients; this should have the consequence of ensuring that the worker will have a forum for her/his own needs (for dependency, nurturance, etc.) to be met, thus lessening the chance that s/he will use the client for this purpose. In general, the well-worn 'know thyself' admonishment for therapists is no less important for being finally unattainable: personal therapy can help clarify one's own beliefs, thoughts and feelings so that they can be used more effectively, helpfully and subversively in therapeutic practice with others.

Although we have argued that supervision is crucial for

good therapeutic practice, it is less clear whether everyone who endeavours to carry out radical therapy has as a matter of course to be in therapy themselves. It may be that some of the functions of personal therapy may be fulfilled by supervision, while more general needs may be met in different ways for different people, for example through particularly supportive relationships or through various kinds of group experiences. Overall, however, it is difficult to see how an appropriate personal therapy can be substituted by other procedures if one is to engage in the kind of therapeutic practice we have described. This raises an awkward issue for socialists committed to free mental health care: under current conditions, advocating personal therapy is, except where self-help therapy groups can substitute, tantamount to advocating that radical workers should go and purchase private treatment. This contradiction is a painful but irrepressible one and may as well be stated baldly: until free therapeutic provision is available to all who require it, there will be situations, notably many training ones, in which it will have to be bought. The abhorrence of this necessity should only increase the vigour with which changes in provision are sought. We reject the traditional psychoanalytic defence of fees in terms of their therapeutic properties as a reactionary rationalisation, and are adamantly opposed to the stratification of therapeutic provision so that only those who can afford to pay fees receive help. It is a clear political struggle to establish that psychological needs are real, and that everyone is entitled to have those needs met by psychotherapy if that should be appropriate. It is thus a crucial activity for socialists to struggle to extend the provision of therapeutic facilities that are available as of right to all those who wish to make use of them.

It is important to stress at this point that the critical practice we are working towards can never be posed as an alternative to mainstream political activity, through socialist parties, trade unions, feminist campaigns, black organisations, etc. In fact the opposite is true. The development of radical therapy must arise out of a wider political awareness and practice, just as it will also inform it. Similarly, we are not proposing therapy as an universal panacea, or imagining some absurd ideal world in which everyone has their own therapist: obviously, large political changes can only come about through social movements, as can any major diminution in the level of human suffering.

Our discussion has employed psychoanalytic concepts and advocated psychoanalytically influenced methods of working. This is not to suggest that everyone needs a full five-times-per-week analysis, nor would that model be appropriate to most of the settings in which mental health workers find themselves. It *is* the case that psychoanalysis in conjunction with political analysis can be applied fruitfully to explain many of the processes determining the whole range of therapeutic encounters and settings. Psychoanalytic theory can be helpful in developing political understanding, and aspects of psychoanalytic practice are relevant to any radical practice – particularly its sensitivity to boundaries and the giving of meaning to apparently senseless phenomena, whether or not an interpretation is actually made.

Our language has been that of the encounter between therapist and individual client. However, most mental health work, not to mention political activity, takes place in groups, as did four of the six illustrations of Chapter 4. In each case 'therapeutic' progress arose from other members of the group as well as from direct interventions by the therapist or group leader (though this is not to say the leader's presence was not significant). One question is whether what occurs in groups can be understood using the same concepts as with individuals. The illustrations show, for example, that the dominance of ideological constructs, internalisation of dominant discourses or repression of problematic needs and desires can all be observed in the functioning of groups, perhaps even more extremely than with individuals. In addition, the aim of subverting common-sense assumptions and the use of subjectification to calibrate the extent to which this is achieved apply as strongly to groups. A second question, though, is whether the straightforward therapist-client model takes sufficient account of the wider ideological and political configurations within which mental health practice takes place, whether it concentrates too much on the micro-social detail at the expense of the macro-social context. Our response is to distinguish between radical *therapy* and radical *mental health practice*. The latter includes the former but is not co-extensive with it. It is true that radical therapy is particularly concerned with the politics of the minutiae of human interaction. However, as we have tried to show, the principles behind radical therapy are of relevance both to mental health practice and to politics as a whole. In Chapter 6, we move away from a narrow concern with the principles of radical therapy to examine the wider social and political context in which mental health work takes place, paying particular attention to the fashionable and apparently progressive enterprise of developing a 'community strategy' for mental health.

6
The Community Strategy

Throughout this book we have concentrated on the ideology and theory that informs therapeutic work, for the most part using examples from practical settings which emphasise individual, family or group processes. We have also argued that power is the central issue in therapeutic work and that the production of power depends not simply on the attributes of the powerful but also on how power relations are internalised and come to act as a form of self-control. Power is not identical with control and oppression, and the stance taken up with respect to power may determine the changes that are possible for both client and therapist. Broadly speaking this chapter is concerned with power and the community. There is a view that the oppressive and bureaucratic nature of the state can be challenged by recourse to community activation, 'community politics', and that this is inherently progressive. We shall argue that this can constitute a kind of fetishism of the community, participating in ideological practices that turn 'the community' into an objectified commodity of capitalism, and relying on a fantasised, idealised 'community' which is a dubious reflection of reality but can have serious political repercussions. We suggest that the 'community strategy' in mental health practice is partly rooted in the ideology of the family and in bourgeois consensus. This does not mean that resistance is never present in the community; rather, the community is not in itself a radical entity, but has a function in the production of ideology and control as well as a potential for resistance – just like any other political space. The apparent consensus of the Left, the Right, social science academics, mental health professionals and the general public on the value of the community is extremely misleading (although such apparent unanimity should itself ring alarm bells for those interested in political change) because it suggests that there is also consensus on what 'the community' is and should be. In fact, there are radical disagreements, symbolized by the way the state's interest in the community has always been in conflict with the interests of those who actually live in these communities – the working class. Yet these disagreements are easily lost in the rhetoric of the community strategy, producing 'the community' as the ideological home of an enormous range of activists of all political persuasions. The attraction and resilience of the community as a target for mental health practice is our starting point.

FETISHISING THE COMMUNITY

The convergence of Left and Right on 'the community' as the vehicle for improved standards of welfare complicates the issue of clarifying what might be a radical intervention in the community. For instance, the commitment by left-wing local councils to community activity shares in practice many similar assumptions to the right-wing, anti-statist stance. Both approaches seek to lead from the top; that is, in spite of sloganising on both sides, neither is a response to working-class pressure. Both approaches adopt a profound suspicion of professional social workers and other welfare workers, albeit for different reasons. Even the Left's commitment to a more visible and accountable service is not always poles apart from the Right's appeal to self-help and freedom of choice. The major difference is that the Left is at least in principle committed to the protection of services, while the Right has as its project the dismantling of the welfare state.

There are many effects of this convergence, two of which stand out for comment. First, the resurrection of the Right's interest in the community has had, by no means for the first time, the effect of depoliticising debate about the community strategy (see Gough, 1979, for a thorough discussion). Second, as in the area of psychological treatments, the Left has lost its chance of taking a political initiative by failing to develop an analysis of the experiences of many workers 'in the community' − powerlessness, apathy, isolation, self-destructiveness, operating both at an organisational and a subjective level. The absence of a full analysis has vacated the field to a range of vague generalisations which, in their appeal to the lost romance of community life, are indistinguishable from the conformist fantasies that we discuss below. The Left has allowed a split to appear between the politics of work and the politics of community action, a split that has been to the cost of both. The traditions of the Left have been to organise predominantly at the place of work, thus colluding with the marginalisation of the unwaged and their relegation to a position of little political value. Not only does this perpetuate a division between work and non-work, with the implication that the place of work has the potential for subversion whilst personal and social relations do not, but has also had the effect of excluding women and the unemployed from the arena of legitimised struggle. This narrowing of the base for struggle has been accentuated by the way the organisations of the community as well as the labour movement have been dominated by men, predominantly white, relegating women, the handicapped, the aged and others who are granted the patronising label 'minority' ('women and other minorities', in media-speak) to trivial activities, while the serious business of planning and negotiation goes to those with experience − men. Not surprisingly, patriarchy in its oppressive and conservative reality has only been challenged in the community by people making connections between their experiences and the need for political action − and these people have not usually been white men. The result is that such community resistance to patriarchal structures has often found itself in opposition to the establishment of the Left.

The Right has usually been explicitly romantic in its approach to the community and community development:

> We are seeking to do through the medium of our local community organisations such things as will get action and interest for the little world of the locality. We are encouraging a new parochialism, seeking to initiate a movement that will run counter to the current romanticism, with its eye

always on the horizon, that is social change; one which will recognise limits, that is the status quo, and work within them.

(Park, 1952, p.179)

Admittedly, this was written some thirty years ago when the ideological purpose of community instruction was more crudely evident than at present. However, much of its message remains intact, and is even coming back into vogue. It contains three major themes that are all being exploited by ideologues of the Right: (a) parochialism, the reduction of the social world to narrow limits, usually geographical ones; (b) reformism, the reduction of what is appropriately considered a target for change; (c) endogeny, the identification of, and response to, problems 'within' the community. Underpinning these themes is an affiliation to a consensus view of change that is applied to community, family and individuals, and which is analogous to the 'breakdown' model described in our first chapter: the social fabric is inherently harmonious, so problems occur only as aberrations. In fact, given the contradictions and conflicts of social life, it is a major ideological job for people to be led to believe that consensus is possible, a job that is carried out in part by precisely the community rhetoric illustrated above. If the world can be reduced to your immediate neighbourhood, if the status quo can be presented as natural necessity, and if the local community can be berated or praised for its performance in controlling 'its' problems, then harmony might appear achievable this side of the rainbow. Baldock shows where this path leads:

> The essential point is that...conflicts of interest are of fundamental importance in all major areas of life in our society and, therefore, full consensus is only possible if people are prepared to restrict themselves to the trivial.
>
> (Baldock, 1974, p.287)

It would be a mistake, however, simply to write off the appeal of the community as an ideological fabrication. For one thing, as we shall discuss at the end of this chapter, the community does hold seeds of resistance which are the source of real optimism about change. But even leaving this aside for the moment, there is something in the 'community' message that has proved to be immensely attractive, an unmistakable resonance that has a powerful hold on many people. This is, in contrast to the explicitness of the right-wing message, a hidden ideological discourse centring on a fantasy which might be called the 'remembered community'. The commitment that many people feel to the notion of community is in large measure symbolic, arising out of the experience of the privatised and alienated reality of everyday life. It is a response to people's perceptions of the quality of their lives, particularly their social relationships, and contains a half-formulated desire for a more collective, supportive social structure. This desire, rather than struggling towards expression in new forms of social arrangement, resorts to history – not the history of objective fact, but of romanticised fantasy which masquerades as common knowledge/common sense when it is not the content of children's picture books. The 'remembered' community is not, has never been, the real community; it has more affinities with the idealised relations of early family life than with any earthly realm. But its assumed characteristics are of importance, because they are widely shared and trumpeted and often distort the perceptions of radicals as well as serving the interests of those who resist progressive change.

There are four main characteristics of the remembered community that define its boundaries reasonably comprehensively. The first of these is size. Communities are small, separated clearly from one another, manageable and coherent. Second, arising from the notion of manageable size, there is an assumption of interpenetration, that everyone speaks the same language, that community members know and understand the familial and social experience of other members – a sense of wholeness. Third, there is a peculiar view of membership, expressed in the idea that a major distinction between the community and other forms of social organisation lies in 'belongingness', in being inextricably bound one to another, sharing responsibility for each other's lives. Fourth, being a member of such a collective suggests that underlying it is the possibility of participation in some common cause that unites and unifies. 'A sense of community', 'community spirit', 'community care': these are the attributes being appealed to in this shared jargon of social work professionals and the conservative Right. At a symbolic level they resonate some meaning, but they obscure as much as they reveal.

There are several possible discourses that structure 'the community' – for example, as a place of struggle, as a religious collaboration – but it is this 'remembered community' that has dominated the discourses of welfare and recent politics. At its base is the perception that a more collective social pattern would have considerable benefits. However, the remembered community is actually an ideological compromise between the desire for collectivity and the constraints of social forces promoting consumerism and individualism which can only be fully exploited at the expense of the community and a more collective way of life. For one thing, it is noticeable that in all the volumes of sociological study, 'the community' is a notion largely applied to the working class; this raises the question of whether its construction serves the purpose of obscuring class, either presenting it as a natural phenomenon (the working-class community slipping nonchalantly into the idealised 'community' of the simple savage in everybody's anthropological imagination) or obscuring oppression by a romantic rewriting of history. Second, it is probably no accident that the elevation of membership and belongingness in community life (there is, of course, much less encouragement to join a trade union) happens at the time when people's experiences of life 'in' their communities is at its most atomised:

> We have moved into a restricted, privatised period of history, in which emotion is distrusted...but in this newly Puritan age, emotion is not being replaced by the light of pure reason – it is being replaced by fear.
>
> (Jones, 1983)

The light of fantasised community belongingness is turned up to outshine the more difficult, but also more realistic, candle of struggle for change in the basic structures of society. Third, there is an implicit image of control in the notion of membership, which may be the area in which the remembered community is closest to the reality of communal life in the past. Membership does not simply mean belonging in a passive sense, but also suggests participating in the project of maintaining the common interest. More strongly, it embraces a notion of consensus which has two particularly powerful conformist attributes. First, it encourages participation with the state and its agencies, so that the common interests within the community are representations of the common interest 'between' the community and the state, which in fact are the interests of the state. Second, membership serves the important function of denying reality status to people who are not in on the consensus – to people who are not 'members'. When reactionary politicians endorse 'Victorian values' and the 'traditional' community, they do so in the full knowledge that these communities were extremely punitive to those who transgressed social norms. To be gay or black, to be a woman: these are not positions from which the remembered community looks so attractive. Membership for some produces exile for others. What is so attractive to the Right about the remembered community is that it softens their basic message and makes it palatable: in an important sense, these communities produced their own forms of social control, alongside the control exercised through labour and the institutions of the state.

The remembered community reflects a paradigm of community life that is perpetuated in various forms by the communications media, politicians and welfare workers alike. The very process of remembering takes place within the context of forces which devastate memory by turning it to their own account: memory occurs in the present, informed by those ideas that have currency in the present. Common sense tells us that the community is a good thing; this message is reinforced in television soap operas and academic studies of working-class life; its appeal is reinforced, too, by the experience of individualism which too often turns out to be the lonely, fearful, powerless product of living in the community. This is not to say that there are no positive elements in community activity, that communities cannot be the focus for radical work; the point is that the remembered community serves specific interests and forms a dominant discourse in political and welfare work which does not contain the seeds of this more progressive activity. Part of the ideological practice of the Left has to be to construct its own discourse, its image of community care which opposes the romanticising of past oppressions in the interests of present ones. One way to begin to re-read the community is to realise just how it has been constructed by political processes and – more particularly for our subject – just what the reality of community care is all about.

THE PENETRATION OF COMMUNITY LIFE

Everyday life is dominated by relations of power and the concomitant production of points of resistance. For the purposes of this discussion, two nodal points for power relations are of particular significance in terms of their influence on the community, namely work and the state. Work has tremendous importance, both materially and symbolically, in providing a barometer of social position and value. It is associated with rationality, order and purpose, subjective values that are internalised to create what is experienced as a moral duty to work. The presence or absence of work has a major impact on the dynamics and culture of a community, as does the nature of whatever work is available. The escalation of unemployment not only breaks down communities in material terms, as people become impoverished or move away, but it undermines the assumptions of purpose and stability that support the experience of community coherence.

The second nodal point for power relations is the state. The experiences of everyday life have been dramatically influenced by the activity of the state, 'from the cradle to the grave', sickness and health, education, welfare, income-maintenance, transport, the police; the state's proximity to our lives is inescapably close. For those most dependent on the state – the very young, the old, the sick, the unemployed – the relationship with the state is like that of an employee to a boss. Whereas the latter relationship is mediated by the product and the search for profit, the former is mediated by the production of social discipline. For the wholly dependent, in terms of income, a sense of dignity, self-respect and internal order will depend on how well they do at their work of extracting the most for themselves and their families from a reluctant state, and this in turn will vary with their relationship to social discipline, to the maintenance of an ordered and predictable position within the network of approved social relationships. State welfare has benefits that improve the quality of all our lives significantly and importantly; however, it also operates in the interests of certain social arrangements:

> Although the State may appear to protect us from the worst excesses of capitalism, it is in fact protecting capital from our strength by ensuring that we relate to capital and to each other in ways which divide us from ourselves, and leave basic inequalities unquestioned.
> (London-Edinburgh Weekend Return Group, 1979, p.2)

The commitment to welfare is most pronounced at the time the working class is most clamorous and angry. If other forces can produce social control – e.g. unemployment – then the shallowness of the commitment to welfare can be seen for what it is.

Within working-class communities a major dynamic has always been a powerful competition between, on the one hand, subversiveness informed by class consciousness and, on the other, conservatism informed by the family and patriarchal relations. State intervention has quite explicitly reinforced the latter at the expense of the former. It is important that this point is recognised, for the community strategy has itself been based on the family as the basic unit of the community, not its class. The community has been transformed by the changing demands of capital and the consequent changes in the nature of state control: 'The State, like a corporation, looks for ways of influencing the environment so that its own present or future behaviour is more efficient' (Ackoff, 1970, p.100). One of the ways in which this is achieved is by

> integrating the local population into predictable 'families' and 'community groups' and by setting up 'joint commit-

tees' between itself and them so that the State can develop a level of information flow that amounts to 'governance'.

(Cockburn, 1977, p.100).

This is not, of course, a new process. It was the fear of the unity between the workplace and the community, which was encouraged by the nineteenth-century British Labour movement, that prompted the state to intervene by developing welfare services. The policy of the Charity Organisation Society was a classic example of how state intervention purports to be about the delivery of caring services but has the effect of fragmenting the working class and its organisations. Its attempt to distinguish between the deserving and the undeserving poor was coupled with the thrust to 'scientise' welfare as a means of controlling those services. In effect, this meant the imposition of an ideological view of poverty and distress that was individually rather than class-based, and which aimed to delegitimise the organisations of the working class. But it is arguable that the penetration of ordinary life by the state has reached a high point in late capitalism, with its desire for the subjective needs of people as well as their objective labour to be used in the service of capital. Late capitalism suffers continually under the possibility of stagnation due to the swamping of markets by commodities. Kovel identifies its response:

Capitalism adapts to the threat by a host of interrelated devices, three of which may be schematically set out here…
(1) an emphasis on the consumption of commodities
(2) increasing technical control of the human input into the production process
(3) in order to secure (1) and (2) a more or less systematic attempt to penetrate and control everyday life, including subjectivity.

(Kovel, 1981, p.75)

Since the war industry has changed progressively from being labour-intensive to being capital-intensive, and from early capitalism to late capitalist multinational industries. In spite of the apparent affluence of the 1950s and 1960s, the seeds of a larger transformation had been sown, the full effects of which have only been felt as international capital has lumbered from boom to stagnation to crisis. Community life has suffered drastically as a result, most importantly from the fracturing of the link between work and life produced by urban de-industrialisation. The effect of this process has been felt not just in the availability of work but also in a shift from the extended to the nuclear family structure, and in changes in working-class culture. But most significantly there has been a shift in the nature of the control exerted by the state over the community, with everyday life being managed more com-pletely in the interests of social discipline. As Kovel points out, this control has increasingly taken the form of the management of subjectivity, and one of its major arms has been the 'mental health industry'.

The state has had an interest in the content and form of the urban community since at least the beginning of the industrial revolution, but it can be argued that the intensity of this interest has escalated in recent years. Since the end of the 1950s there has been a parade of reports and commissions advocating one form or another of community strategy in welfare. What unites these strategies is the view that the involvement of the community will produce a less bureaucra-tic and cheaper service on the one hand, and a more humane and progressive service on the other. At the same time, the dominant ideological purpose of welfare – the maintenance of the social order – will remain intact. When transformed into practice, the orientation of these advocacies becomes even clearer. In the 1980s the community strategy has contributed to a much more substantial shift than previously away from a commitment to the provision of welfare. Essentially, the policies of community care represent a transfer of care and support from the state to the family; it is in effect a transfer of dependency, the burden of which falls upon women. It is one thing to argue for the self-activity of local people around issues or activities of their own choosing; it is quite another for the state in effect to colonise the community and transfer its activity on to the 'caring local networks'. The combination of this process, plus rising unemployment (which has also fallen disproportionately hard on women) is increasingly having the effect of forcing women to remain at home: when nursery places, hospital beds and old people's homes disappear, it is women at home who pick up the pieces. If you are mentally ill in the community you are likely to be a woman or be looked after by a woman, or you will be alone. As the large psychiatric hospitals close their back wards, so patients who have become depersonalised and institutionalised by the hospital system are discharged into a system of community care in relation to which they are quite marginal and about which they are rightly scared and uncomprehending. At a time of cuts and deteriorating services all round, only one half of the community strategy is adhered to in any case: the half that involves closing down hospitals and other institutional arrangements. Building up real community alternatives is less popular, as various surveys have shown (e.g. Shepherd, 1984).

There are two central aspects to this process that warrant discussion, in terms of their ideological underpinnings as much as the stark reality of the crumbling services which they often represent. The first of these comes loosely within the framework of care 'by' the community, the second of care 'in' it.

First, the rhetoric of 'the community' hides another rhetoric, that of family life. In practice it is women who carry the burden of the implementation of community strategies. Ideologically, the romantic fantasy of the remembered community is identical with the romantic fantasy of the family, associated symbolically with security, warmth and continuous care, obscuring issues of class, race and gender, claiming the role of the basic unit of social organisation. As we discussed in Chapter 1, where welfare operates, it merges subtly with internalised images of family care, translating professional roles into family ones – doctor and nurse, father and mother. The alienated and fragmented social relations of capitalism are made manageable by the fact and fiction of the caring family: the fact because, with all its oppressive elements, it is in the family that most people receive their only experiences of care; the fiction because this experience is used ruthlessly to undermine the mobilisation of oppressed people around welfare struggles, to fragment, to reduce politics to inadequacies in self-help. Welfare state and citizen, doctor and patient, parent and child: these are the ideological emblems of caring called into operation in the community strategy as in other instances of welfare politics. Their net result is the reproduction of dominant social relations through the articulation only of dominant discourses, in this case the discourses that place the community and the family together in the realm of 'natural' social structures, and the motif of care in the image of the maternal embrace. 'The community', in this way, can become a significant link in a system that prevents real alternative forms of helping relationship from developing.

The second point concerning the ideological underpinnings of the community strategy is connected to the problems of constructing community resources to deal with people with varying needs. Specifically, the notion that people who have been chronically disturbed or institutionalised for many years should be 'normalised' is questionable. The movement of mental health services away from the large hospital and into the community is well under way: between 1954 and 1979 the number of residents of mental hospitals in England and Wales fell from about 150,000 to 76,000. However, it is only relatively recently that the closure of these hospitals has been seriously contemplated, and with it has developed a dual interest in the 'rehabilitation' of current residents and the systematic provision of resources for them in the community. Although, as has already been mentioned, it must be said that the response of 'the community', as measured either by its residents or its 'representatives' in local and central government, has not been one of wild enthusiasm, it is not sufficient to dismiss this development as a subtle manoeuvre of the state to offload responsibility for some of its most disabled citizens. On the contrary, the move towards community care does represent an advance, one heavily influenced by the criticisms of Goffman and his followers in the 1950s and 1960s. If we are to come to a critical understanding of it, the underlying assumptions of rehabilitation practice must be examined.

There is a large technical literature on psychiatric rehabilitation, concerned with such issues as which practices are appropriate to which groups of patients, the different sets of factors that determine the quality of institutional care, the problems of institutional change, and so on. At the most general level, though, its development can be seen as a progressively more sophisticated elaboration of the related principles of 'de-institutionalisation' and 'normalisation' of patients, staff and services. Thus it is recognised that the drab, uniform mass treatments of the old mental hospital tended to strip the patient of basic human skills and individuality, and that what is needed is on the one hand to repair that process in so far as is possible with long-stay chronic patients, and on the other hand to plan a service that lacks those characteristics, ensuring that the mistakes of the past are not repeated. Reparation involves re-individualising patients, enabling them to have personal possessions, treating them as individuals with rights and abilities, offering training in basic 'normal' skills such as the handling of money, cooking, shopping and leisure activities – a process of re-socialisation. Correspondingly, the planning of services is carried out with an eye to ensuring that the patient leads as normal a life as possible. These are worthy aims, not at all easy to achieve, and while we wish to make some criticisms, these are not intended to detract from the genuine concern of those working in this area. A more detailed overview than can be provided here is to be found in Shepherd (1984) and Watts and Bennett (1984).

The first point to note is that the principle of normalisation, while not directly subject to the charge that it is trying to punish deviance or turn people into faceless 'normals' (for see the conditions *from* which people are being normalised) takes no account of the forces that operated to produce the state of affairs that is supposedly being rectified. In addition, it does not acknowledge the advantages of institutional arrangements for patients, staff and the community at large. At its most naive, it thus assumes that everyone can be persuaded to recognise how much better it is to treat people humanely in normal, non-institutional settings. Although workers might acknowledge that this is not as straightforward as it sounds, resistance is seen as largely irrational, due to prejudice and traditionalism, rather than as the product of forces that are still very much alive today. As we argued in Chapter 1, the treatment of patients goes on within a complex power structure with both subjective and objective components that quite understandably resist change, because change is a real threat to them. For example, the dominance of the medical model in psychiatry is clearly threatened by an approach that suggests that the primary need of the patient is to be treated with dignity and respect; staff are likely to feel highly threatened by the possibility that they may have to confront the anxieties generated by severely disturbed individuals; patients and staff are likely to feel threatened by the possibility of 'taking back' some of those aspects of themselves that have been split off and projected into those around them; and the community at large is understandably reluctant to live with an acknowledgement of psychotic anxieties, rather than locating them in the hospital, outside their daily lives. By ignoring these factors the normalisation model fails to challenge the structures that produce the situation supposedly being undermined, and creates the conditions under which rehabilitation can be seen as an adjunct to the medical model. Drugs plus rehabilitation is now the prescription; better than drugs alone, it continues to reify distress as illness. Thus the 'return to the community' of mental health services and patients is a return in an alienated form: the community receives back a part of itself in a form not recognisable as having belonged, or as still belonging, to the community. This is very different from the concept of subjectification discussed in Chapter 5, which involves a taking back that re-integrates that which has become unintelligible or split off.

Our next criticism relates to the point just made: the principle of normalisation, although it does imply the participation of the community in the planning process, fails to recognise the effects of the imposition of community care on people from above. It is well known that it is extremely hard to get 'the community' involved in 'their' service, a difficulty easily ascribed to passivity when in fact it reflects the lack of control actually given to people in planning these services. The 'involvement of local people', while not without positive potential, is also a further twist of the spiral of dependence on the welfare state, a formalisation of existing power relations rather than a transfer of power. In the same way as a scheme to involve the unemployed in determining how much benefit they should receive might be better than current bureaucratic practice but would also formalise their dependence on the state's power to offer work or subsistence, so the imposition of community mental health services formalises the community's powerlessness to change things enough to deal with its 'mental illness'. Definitions of illness and health, insanity and sanity, are retained in this approach to treatment in the community; all that has happened is that the community has been pulled into active involvement with the network of these definitions, subordinate to them and acting in their name.

KNOWLEDGE AND CONTROL

In the preceding section we have been critical of the community strategy in mental health care because (a) it is by no means necessarily a route to improved services, (b) it oppresses women, and (c) it contributes to the ideological retreat from welfare. Most of all, we have emphasised how it feeds into the dominant discourses surrounding the current organisation of power relations, particularly by linking up with discourses on the family to produce a conformist axis for mental health interventions. The geographical move of services into the community and the increase in care by the community do not in themselves promote subjectification. Nevertheless, this does not mean that the community should be written off as a source of struggle and a space within which to construct a radical practice. It is simply that the discourses that create reactionary community practice must be challenged by discourses identifying the progressive possibilities in community activation.

The perpetuation of conformist ideology in the context of community mental health is closely bound up with the power of the state to define the boundaries of rational practice. It is not a simple matter of the state taking further control in order to maintain the status quo, for the community strategy can involve progress in the quality of care and offer the chance of strengthening local involvement. There is no simple relationship between the state and the citizen whereby the latter is either cared for or controlled by the former. What does exist is the penetration of everyday life by state structures that create enormous difficulties for workers attempting to take a new grasp of the language of mental health activity and twist it into the semblance of radical resistance: 'Capitalism has severed the ties of personal dependence only to revive dependence under the guise of bureaucratic rationality' (Lasch, 1982, p.359).

Rationality does not refer, as many community strategists might suggest, only to the organisational form of the welfare state, but much more importantly to the state's claim to be the legitimate interpreter of reality. As the various arms of the state have developed, so they have laid claim to expertise that has given them the substantial influence that accrues to those with special knowledge, by definition more than is available to the lay person. Knowledge has, in effect, been colonised by the professions as a way of distinguishing themselves from other bodies. Their practice, however, is sanctioned, legitimised and paid for by the state. It is this dependent relationship that ensures that professional knowledge is for the most part inscribed within the arc of what is congruent with the activity of the state, is even put to the use of the state. Just as the interactions between patients and doctors service the ideology of passivity and individualism (see Chapter 1), so the power of interpretation invested in 'knowledge experts' such as professional organisations, academics and politicians has important implications for social and personal control:

> The popular tradition of self-reliance has, in effect, been converted into esoteric knowledge administered by experts, which has helped the growing belief that everyday life is too complex and lies beyond the reach of ordinary people.
> (Lasch, 1982, p.226)

'Knowledge experts' are influential partly because of their positions within the state apparatus as managers, consultants, researchers and policy-makers, and partly because their knowledge is reinforced and used by 'action experts' – family doctors, teachers, social workers, local government officers, psychiatrists. These 'action experts' are themselves dependent on 'knowledge experts' for their status and employment, at least in their initial and continued accreditation, and often more directly than that. Thus the services offered to the users of welfare are contained within the parameters of acceptable knowledge, over which the user has little control. Control is exercised by the state through its experts, not simply by their capacity to ration the delivery and quality of services, but also because of the nature of the services; as described earlier, this expertise endorses the dominant ideology, most notably in connection with the family and patriarchal relations. Finally, the impact of experts is to bring knowledge into fewer and fewer hands and then frequently to distort it. As Jacoby (1975) has argued, the use of knowledge is predominantly to legitimise the present, to rework the past so that it can be accommodated into present ideological assumptions, and to rob the past of its materiality and hence of its subversive potential:

> Exactly because the past is forgotten, it rules unchallenged; to be transcended it must first be remembered. Social amnesia is society's repression of remembrance – society's own past. It is a psychic commodity of the commodity society.
>
> (Jacoby, 1975, p.5)

As in our description of the 'remembered community' earlier in this chapter, the ideological status of common-sense assumptions has to be demonstrated in order to create the conditions for the establishment of resistance. Expertise in the area of mental health is commonly used in the interests of alienation, whether of the individual or of the community. Its function is frequently to prevent the re-integration of dismembered existence; its activity is defensive and explicitly or ultimately conformist. In the generation of resistance, the first point concerns the return of knowledge to the community – not in the form of the fetishised fossils of common sense, but as an attitude to power, to the assertion of subversiveness in everyday life.

RESISTANCE

The community contains the potential both for resistance (based on class consciousness and struggle) and conformism (based on the family and patriarchal relations). In ways discussed earlier, the latter tendency is reinforced at the expense of the former, but it is never able to claim a complete and sustained victory. In every imposition of control the seeds of resistance are sown; the operation of power produces its own negation. Resistance to the daily oppressiveness of the modern, alienated community and to the presence of the state in everyday life continually asserts itself, ranging in form from vandalism (analogous to self-mutilation) to conscious political struggle of the kind observable in the response of pit villages and miners' wives to the 1984 British miners' strike. Often resistance is restricted to the activity of defiance, a stubborn refusal to bow to control rather than to attempt to subvert it. Defiance of this kind is everywhere, with a major question for the community activist being how to transform it into radical action. In this respect the process of subjectification is as relevant to action within the community as it is to more explicitly therapeutic work, precisely because it is rooted in an understanding of the relationshjp between experience and structure, which is both individual and collective. By revealing the principles that determine the shape of people's experiences in the social world, radical action to subvert these principles becomes possible.

Various community mental health projects have been instituted in recent years in Britain, but in spite of being progressive when compared with what has gone before, they all, to a greater or lesser extent, reproduce the orthodox medical hierarchy and stop short of challenging the content of services to the 'mentally ill'. The ideologically 'neutral' stance taken by so many proponents of community mental health ensures that even if the process of deinstitutionalisation continues to its logical end, it will not produce a radical service. The major reformist document produced by the Association for Mental Health (MIND) is particularly revealing of the limitations of this kind of approach. In *Common Concern* (MIND, 1983) an argument is put forward for a comprehensive approach to mental health care, but the ambition of these proposals is stated as being to

(1) enhance citizenship for all those who have suffered or are suffering from mental illness; (2) reduce or eliminate

the inequalities which are inevitably created through the experience of mental illness.

The report goes on to say:

> The key to achieving these objectives will be an acceptance throughout the new mental health service of the right of the *individual* to appropriate care.

These are obviously worthy aims, but they are not radical ones; they are more akin to civil liberties campaigns arguing for the rights of individuals than to a programme for a restructuring of attitudes to psychological distress. The existence of mental illness is taken as given, as are the legitimacy of current treatments; the aim is simply to make sure that individuals suffering from the former get the best possible exposure to the latter. Our argument against this position is twofold. First, politics does not end at the consulting-room door: therapy of all kinds is a political procedure, trading in power relations and reflecting the giant structuring principles of society in the most intimate of micro-social encounters. It is not just the packaging of treatments that needs to be subverted, but their content. Second, the consistent emphasis in reformist documents on individual treatments will hopefully produce a more humane and respectful psychiatric service, but does not even begin to develop an understanding of those factors that are collectively experienced and which impinge on the mental health of everyone. The huge numbers of people that receive some kind of help for psychological difficulties – usually a prescription for drugs – attest to the way such difficulties have acquired epidemic standing. Under these circumstances it is important to include in any mental health strategy an investigation of the normality of psychological distress: that is, one is brought back time and again to the social factors that construct and produce suffering. A comprehensive policy must, of course, offer help to people in acute distress and also to those suffering from chronic difficulties, and this help must be appropriate to their needs, in much the way that the MIND proposals suggest. But restricting consideration to certain defined patients maintains the split between health and illness that ensures that mental health services remain separated from everyday life. It is not simply services that need to be moved to the community, but the whole concept of mental health itself. If we were to design a manifesto to parallel that of MIND, it would be couched at a less individualistic level, one geared to an emphasis on the needs of all community members rather than just those afflicted with psychiatric labels. For instance, a community mental health service should be available to all who wish to use it; it should be concerned with the maintenance and promotion of positive mental health as well as with the remediation of distress; it should provide services at all places in the community where the need arises (home, school, workplace, union, etc.); it should attempt to develop an indigenous service for all subgroups, especially women and minority national and class groups; and it should be responsive to the needs of the community, not just in being managed by community members but in actively campaigning on behalf of the community, that is, in getting involved in politics. In this way, it would be oriented towards uniting the experiences of social and personal subjugation, demonstrating the links that sustain their co-presence and provide the sources of activity that subvert them both.

Our major criticism of reformist work is its ideological naivety: in withdrawing from political struggle in every arena except that of civil liberties it creates an illusion of liberal consensus, where what is in fact occurring is an endorsement of current perceptions and strategies of control. Resistance does not flow naturally from the imposition of services on the community. Where it does appear is in activation, struggle on specific issues which turn out to structure people's social experiences and hence their 'mental health'. Most community interventions have addressed this only indirectly. For instance, Sedgwick (1982) refers to a number of radically inspired 'mental illness' interventions such as those of the Groupes Information Asiles in France and the Mental Patients' Union in Britain, correctly pointing out that they have been concerned more with establishing greater patient control over existing psychiatric facilities than constructing a new approach to mental health. On the other hand, those movements arising out of the anti-psychiatric critiques of the 1960s provide little to help people suffering from chronic or very severe psychological difficulties. Sedgwick's concluding example, a sympathetic portrait of the Belgian town of Geel which Kropotkin originally produced to exemplify the power of voluntary social initiatives, itself begs a number of important questions. Certainly the 'normalisation' of psychiatric patients is achieved to an impressive extent, and relationships are formed that appear to have the potential for revising the community's notion of mental illness as much as they improve the quality of the life of people who might otherwise be institutionalised. In addition, the support for care-giving which members of the town offer one another is an important instant of good practice for services located 'in' the community. However, there is a crucial limitation to the viability of Geel as a prototype for radical community mental health practice. It is only after being categorised as psychiatrically disturbed that people are sent to Geel, and once there they subsist within the constraints imposed by recognition of their special status – Sedgwick mentions, for instance, that there is strict prohibition of sexual contact between patients and that there is also extensive limiting of unaccompanied trips to the town (p.254). The townsfolk who take on the job of looking after people are paid for their labours: this is obviously appropriate, but it also highlights the sense in which the town is simply being used as a superior and apparently more humane form of long-stay treatment than traditional psychiatric institutions. The goings-on at Geel do little to challenge the psychiatric discourses that construct psychological distress as a disease state that separates some people from others; it is not an example of community mental health, only of community care.

Another intervention considered by Sedgwick involves some rather different principles and possibilities. This is the reforms generated in the Italian psychiatric service by the Psychiatria Democratica movement (Basaglia, 1981; Ramon, 1983). This movement has had remarkable successes in democratising psychiatric institutions and in making mental health care a political topic of major importance. In particular, the endorsement of Psychiatria Democratica's ideas in the

Mental Health Act of 1978, especially concerning the closure of traditional mental hospitals and the provision of alternative community resources, was an unprecedented achievement for a radical mental health movement. This is not the place to discuss the Italian experience in any great detail, but it is worth pointing out one major similarity and one major difference to our own approach. First, Psychiatria Democratica do not regard it as sufficient simply to make the implementation of psychiatric technology more humane. Instead, they challenge the inequalities of psychiatric treatment and the assumptions on which they are based, particularly those concerning professional roles and the nature of 'mental illness': 'illness is seen essentially as a distorted representation of specific contradictions of the subject in his social relations' (Basaglia, 1981, p.190).

In terms of community involvement, although the practice of the reforms is often limited to the provision of community walk-in centres which provide counselling and practical help, it is clear that much of the intention and central struggle of the movement lies in radicalising the community's perceptions of psychological disturbance in line with Psychiatria Democratica's own perspective. However, it is also apparent that the movement holds to a strong anti-therapy position, on the grounds that therapy individualises and privatises the experiences of people which should instead be located in their social relationships. Our own position is that this promotes a false individual–social dichotomy which limits the potential radicalness of any intervention by failing to address the unconscious internalisation of social structures. Therapy and community involvement need to go together to allow a fundamental change in the politics of mental health to occur.

Resistance is produced in the operation of power: without power there is no resistance; alongside the exercise of power there is always opposition. At the level of individual therapy, this means that the exposure and exploration of power struggles can convert therapy into a subversive enterprise directed at overturning the internalised precipitates of social structures. But it also applies at the level of the community. The real community is not like the 'remembered' one. It is a divided place, split along lines of class, gender and race; it is not through ignoring these divisions but through surmounting them in active struggle that opposition can be made coherent. The everyday nature of psychological distress is relevant here, the way it is part of each person's experience. The operation of the state and of the mental health industry that in some respects is its arm is to deny this everydayness, to invest distress with the private quality of abnormality, the connotations of madness. Distress, however, is not a private matter at all, but is generated in and through the social domain. Every manifestation of power is of relevance to mental health, as is every instance of resistance to this power. Thus, a community mental health strategy cannot concern itself simply with providing more accessible treatment services to people already categorised as 'mentally ill'. It must also take up those struggles that influence the quality of mental health: struggles around work, housing, child-care and health care, battles against sexism and racism. This is not just because these struggles are good things in themselves (which they are); nor is it a statement of the impossibility of bringing about changes of any kind except through direct political action. It is rather that these struggles represent opposition to those elements of oppression which link community deprivation and psychological distress. Opposition of this kind moves the community strategy away from a traditional responsive role, operating only when breakdowns in well-being are recognised and 'clients' created, towards a more active assault on the conditions that give rise to psychological suffering. The promotion of positive mental health is a well-worn phrase in preventive psychology, but when 'mental health' is extended to include the subjectificatory experience of challenging the dominance of oppressive forces, it becomes a political slogan. That there are very few examples of community mental health interventions that take on the kind of active political role that we are suggesting is a statement of its difficulty, both practically and conceptually. That there are any interventions which have made the specific struggles of communities part of their programme for mental health attests to the possibilities for action – for there have been and are such interventions, some in the American community mental health movement (see Castel, Castel and Lovell, 1982), and some fairly isolated projects in Europe and Britain (e.g. The Battersea Action and Counselling Centre, described in Bender, 1976).

In this chapter we have criticised the fantasy of the 'remembered' community and the reality of the community strategies that have arisen with it. We have argued that community projects have at best been limited to attempts to improve the quality of care given to people designated as psychiatrically disturbed; at worst, they have partaken of a reactionary ideology pushing the burdens of care back on to families and particularly women. Finally, we have stressed the importance of resistance to oppression at all points where it impinges on the 'mental health' of communities and of the individuals within them. These points are recognisable in the ordinary instances of political action within communities, but are not usually made part of a community mental health intervention. But community mental health does not mean simply re-siting services. It means a broad recognition of the pervasive operations of the power structures that create distress and opposition to them at every point at which they have an impact. Leonard (1984) draws attention to the direct effects that such collective action can have on mental health and personal well-being: for example by opposing dominant individualistic discourses and encouraging 'socialist altruism', by developing people's personal capacities through the needs of effective struggle, and -most significantly- by the way involvement in collective activity may lead to the internalisation of an altered conception of the self 'whereby subordinacy is resisted through the incorporation of alternative meanings and definitions, including altering conceptions of what is possible in terms of change, in other words a raising of consciousness' (p.118).

As Leonard suggests, whether one is an adherent of Sève's (1978) position that changes in consciousness are only fully brought about through revolutionary changes in the material relations of production, or whether, as we do, one follows the arguments of feminists and Gramscians that the dominance of ruling class, patriarchal and racist discourses must also be opposed by ideological struggle, the significance of collective action remains central. Through economic, political and ideological struggle on each specific instance of oppression, what can be called a 'culture of opposition' (London—Edinburgh Weekend Return Group, 1979) can be established, a culture which can unite people where alienation and individualism is otherwise dominant. Resistance is thus a total activity and a precise one, rooted in the experience of community life in the same way that therapy begins from the reality of the split and suffering individual.

Conclusion

The politics of mental health: our title is an invitation to despair in the current climate of politics, with reaction rampant, services constricted, the needy the most punished. Yet we feel that our message in this book is an optimistic one: that there are no natural categories of suffering, that distress is constructed, socialised, that therapeutic practice is a political activity with the potential to reconstruct our discourses on mental health and to contribute to radical struggle. Our orientation has been distinct from that of reformists who have often criticised the inadequacy of mental health services. They are political in their interests only to the extent of having a concern for civil liberties and welfare provision. In their worry over patients' rights (a legitimate worry, of course) they neglect to provide a critique of a person's status as 'patient', or, more formally, of the discourses that give rise to it. Most importantly, they may argue for more humane treatments (less ECT and drugs, for example) but once again this is on the grounds of liberty; there is little analysis of the encounters of treatment, the power relations that are displayed, and what they have to say about psychological distress on the one hand and social malaise on the other. It is precisely the potential for commentary on both internal and public politics that attracts us to the area of mental health. This is the arena where the most forceful encounter occurs between the discourses of the ideological subject and of the subject of the unconscious; in the language of Chapter 5, it allows consideration of both social and psychoanalytic subjectification; put more simply, it deals with the intertwined realities of private and public experience. Politics is both intrinsic and extrinsic to mental health: it can be found in the power relations that operate within and between individuals, and also in those that determine the shape and structure of mental health activity.

A substantial part of this book has been devoted to the intrinsic politics of therapy, this being probably the most unfamiliar part of our thesis. We have tried to show how social relations become the axes around which individuals become constructed, how 'personality' arises as an element in ideology, the lived relationship with the world. We have also explored the power structures endemic to therapeutic encounters, and examined in examples of our own practice the difficulties of generating and sustaining a radical approach to therapy. Power is there, it does not limit itself to telling us when and where to meet; it infiltrates and manipulates, it is a barrier and a channel. There is no world outside politics, neither the macro world of public life nor the micro world of the caring caress. Radical practice involves grasping hold of this, of taking power and the discourses that surround it and regenerating our perceptions, substituting for blind palliative the integration of social and unconscious forces.

Although our argument has been couched mainly at a level of generality which does not involve specific encounters with fundamental political categories of race, gender and class, extrinsic politics have appeared in various ways, most substantially in Chapter 6. For one thing, there is a strong and repeatedly demonstrated link between social situations and personal distress. This link takes various forms, from the simple fact of the heightened 'risk' for people living under stressful and exploited conditions, through the more subtle idea of the internalisation of social forces into the unconscious to provoke conflict and disturbance, to the more conventional 'politics of mental health' – the pressures and interests that give rise to the organisation of services in particular ways, notably in this case the fetishism of 'community care'. Most of all, we have striven to expose links between the discourses of capitalism and patriarchy on the one hand, and those of personal distress and mental health on the other. We have suggested that capitalism develops in proportion to the extent that it undermines the quality of human relationships. Freud took a pessimistic view of private life even in his day: for him, the goal of psychoanalysis could only be to convert 'hysterical misery' into 'common unhappiness' (Breuer and Freud, 1895). There are still less grounds for optimism today. Roughly one person in ten spends some time as a patient in a psychiatric hospital; the numbers receiving treatment from family doctors are even greater. Treatment is offered mainly for distress that has become unmanageable; statistics relating to hospital admissions and the use of psychotropic drugs indicate the extent of this unmanageable distress; manageable distress is now so pervasive that it can be considered normal – 'common unhappiness'. Unlike approaches that view distress as symptomatic of physical disorder, we see it as indicative of people's troubles. In this light, most of the conventional approaches to psychological disturbance that centre on psychiatry can be seen to 'work' by managing the way in which people express their troubles or, to put it differently, by enabling people to express their troubles in a more manageable fashion. In the short run this can be of help to people; in the long run, however, it leaves their troubles untouched and only helps by rendering their unhappiness mute. Distress is no longer clamorous, insistent or improper; it has been made quiet. Troubles still stir within this quiet, but they are contained within the self; they no longer trouble others. The individual is freed to live a normal life, a life of unhappy silence.

The first task for anyone who wishes to make the quality of human relationships the object of intervention is to break this silence, to make troubles speak again in the reality of their own language. The paradox that is encountered here is a familiar and difficult one: as pressure for change increases, so does the resistance it engenders, not just from state structures but also from the internal opposition that results from the threat of change and the overwhelming power of trouble itself. It is important to understand the hold that is maintained by the kinds of medical discourse which privatise distress and enclose it as 'mental illness'. For example, they share a number of things in common with religious approaches to psychological disorder, in particular by granting 'absolution' to the person in distress, illness here being an equivalent of possession. The appeal is to the passive, non-responsible, compliant part of each of us: 'Don't worry, this has nothing to do with you or the life you lead, there's nothing here for you to sort out. All you have to do is co-operate with the treatment'. In addition, the privatisation of distress, its hiding away outside the community, serves many interests. Apart from appeasing the fears discussed in Chapter 6, it also allows individuals suffering from 'mental illness' to seek help without experiencing shame; intriguingly, the greater visibility of distress encouraged by community resources may actually frighten away people whose internal model is of a rational world where experiences such as their own have no place. Exposing one's difficulties is no easy task; the relative anonymity of, and the dependency generated by, privatised procedures feeds into the retreat from this communality. So we must understand the internal factors supporting the continuation of conformist mental health practice, as well as the vested interests that are also present, and in designing our alternatives, we must also replace the sanctuaries that may be lost.

There are no easy routes to resistance: improvements in mental health practice are difficult to achieve, radical changes are even more problematic, while their attainment will not of itself bring about a revolutionary transformation of society. The psychiatrist as social prophet was an epiphenomenon of 1960s romanticism, seeking salvation from within, the world recovered through self-expression. Our project is more humble, but in being more realistic it is also more difficult. At a time when the forces of reaction threaten to wreck all vestiges of humane living, we are suggesting that it is possible to engage in radical struggle within the ordinary practice of mental health work, struggle that can contribute to the resistance against this upsurge in oppressiveness. The different sections of this book have contained an outline strategy for action. In Chapters 1,2 and 3 we drew attention to the importance of challenging the medical model in psychiatry, an approach that serves the interests of alienation and splitting, which encourages passivity and suspicion and which institutionalises the relations of power that produce discontent themselves. In Chapters 4 and 5 we built on the psychoanalytic model that had been proposed as an alternative, to describe ways in which the practice of therapy in ordinary mental health settings could be transformed in the direction of increased subjectification, this being an ability to uncover for people the social and unconscious forces operating to produce distress. Our argument was that it is the analysis of power relations as they appear in the therapeutic situation that creates the conditions for radical practice. Power cannot be wished away in the false egalitarianism of supportive humanistic practice: it exists in and around the therapeutic encounter, and can be found in the structures that lie inside as well as between individuals. It is the task of therapy to lay this bare and work through the connections that the exposure of power's presence reveals. These connections will be social and personal at the same time; they will concern the deepest structures of personality but also the social structuring that has created these structures. Furthermore, they will not be merely intellectual: it is the peculiar importance of therapeutic encounters that they are deeply felt, that 'insight' is a lived experience which moves further than a false thought–feeling dichotomy. As the analyses in Chapter 4 revealed, it is not sufficient to enter mental health work with the intention of being different, of opposing bourgeois discourses on therapeutic care. It is also necessary to create new discourses that recognise the reality of the actual processes of therapy, but which use these realities to subvert conformist practices. Once again, the clearest way in which this can be attempted is through the use of psychoanalytic procedures employed in the service of restructuring power relations.

In addition to the practice of radical therapy in mental health settings, we have explored in Chapter 6 the use of the community as a place of resistance and change. Although critical of community mental health as it has appeared in contemporary social practice, we have also emphasised the potential of community activation for struggles against the alienation and reification that characterises mental health work. Radical activity is that form of opposition which can subvert fundamental social structures; it is through collective struggle that this opposition can be expressed most loudly. In the end, change can only come about through such collective action; but it is also the case that such action can only come about when both personal and social oppression is recognised and opposed. In bringing this to pass, in revealing the forces that produce distress and personal discord, radical mental health practice can help provide the necessary conditions for wider forms of effective social struggle.

Throughout this book we have stressed the importance of practical activity. In some ways we share in the tendency for political activists to react to the recent advances of reaction by turning inwards, becoming absorbed in psychoanalysis as a way of rescuing the quality of one's own and other people's lives, and of explaining the dominance of oppressive ideologies. This is the charge always levelled against therapy by the Left: that it represents a retreat into individualism and creates a silence around social suffering. We have in part attempted to avert this possibility by focusing on action; refusing to take refuge in theory, we have exposed our own work to scrutiny and endorsed some specific modes of practice within an area that we regard as crucial for advances both for individuals and for the social collective. But we also go further than pointing apologetically to our political consciences. Mental health practice operates at a nodal point in the social fabric, where individuals are penetrated by the determining structures of their society. Our perceptions of mental health are not just significant for the way they may alter therapeutic activity, but also because in reconstructing mental health we are also arguing for the importance of an altered understanding of political phenomena. In radicalising therapy and community care, mental health workers can do more than provide better services. They can also challenge assumptions concerning the distribution of power relationships, and the forms that political struggle can take. Most significantly and subversively, they can overturn the discourses which relegate suffering and elation, pain and well-being – all the forces of subjectivity – to the private arena of the unspoken truth. Instead, radicalising mental health can mean making public what is hidden, making open and generous what is confined, and making political what has been reduced to personal, silent pain.

References

Ackoff, R. L. (1970) *A Concept of Corporate Planning* (Chichester: Wiley Interscience).

Althusser, L. (1965) *For Marx* (London: Verso).

Axline, V. (1964) *Dibs: In Search of Self* (London: Victor Gallancz).

Baldock, P. (1974) *Community Work and Social Work* (London: Routledge & Kegan Paul).

Barnes, M. & Berke, J. (1971) *Mary Barnes: Two Accounts of a Journey Through Madness* (Harmondsworth: Penguin).

Basaglia, F. (1981) 'Breaking the Circuit of Control', in Ingleby D., (ed.) *Critical Psychiatry* (Harmondsworth: Penguin).

Beck, A. (1976) *Cognitive Therapy and the Emotional Disorders* (New York: Meridian).

Bender, M. P. (1976) *Community Psychology* (London: Methuen).

Bion, W. R. (1962) 'A Theory of Thinking', *International Journal of Psycho-Analysis*, No. 43.

Bion, W. R. (1967) *Second Thoughts* (London: Heinemann).

Brever, J. and Freud, S. (1895) *Studies on Hysteria* (Harmondsworth: Penguin).

Brown, G. & Harris, T. O. (1978) *Social Origins of Depression* (London: Tavistock).

Brown N. O. (1959) *Life Against Death: The Psychoanalytic Meaning of History* (Connecticut: Wesleyan University Press).

Castel, R., Castel, F. & Lovell, A. (1982) *The Psychiatric Society* (New York: Columbia University Press).

Chodorow, N. (1978) *The Reproduction of Mothering* (Berkeley: University of California Press).

Clare, A. (1976) *Psychiatry in Dissent* (London: Tavistock).

Cochrane, R. & Stopes-Roe, M. (1981) 'Women, Marriage, Employment and Mental Health', *British Journal of Psychiatry*, No. 139, pp. 373–81.

Cockburn, C. (1977) *The Local State: Management of Cities and People* (London: Pluto).

Colletti, L. (ed.) (1978) *Marx: Early Writings* (Harmondsworth: Penguin).

Cooper, D. (1972) *The Death of the Family* (Harmondsworth: Penguin).

Corrigan, P. & Leonard, P. (1978) *Social Work Practice Under Capitalism: A Marxist Approach* (London: Macmillan).

Coulter, J. (1973) *Approaches to Insanity* (London: Martin Robertson).

Coward, R. & Ellis, J. (1977) *Language and Materialism* (London: Routledge & Kegan Paul).

Eichenbaum, L. & Orbach, S. (1982) *Outside In … Inside Out* (Harmondsworth: Penguin).

Engels, F. (1968) 'The Origins of the Family, Private Property and the State', in *Marx & Engels Selected Works* (London: Lawrence & Wishart).

Ernst, S. & Goodison, L. (1967) *In Our Own Hands* (London: The Women's Press).

Foucault, M. (1967) *Madness and Civilisation* (London: Tavistock).

Foucault, M. (1973) *Birth of the Clinic* (London: Tavistock).

Foucault, M. (1977) *Language, Counter-Memory and Practice* (Ithaca, New York: Cornell University Press).

Foucault, M. (1979) *History of Sexuality, Vol. 1* (Harmondsworth: Penguin).

Gallop, J. (1982) *Feminism and Psychoanalysis: The Daughter's Seduction* (London: Macmillan).

Gear, M. C., Hill M. A. & Liendo, M. (1981) *Working Through Narcissism: Treating its Sadomasochistic Structure* (New York: Jason Aronson).

Gramsci, A. (1971) *Prison Notebooks* (London: Lawrence & Wishart).

Gough, I. (1979) *Political Economy of the Welfare State* (London: Macmillan).

Hirst, P. (1979) *On Law and Ideology* (London: Macmillan).

Hirst, P. & Woolley, P. (1982) *Social Relations and Human Attributes* (London: Tavistock).

Jacoby, R. (1975) *Social Amnesia: A Critique of Conformist Psychology from Adler to Laing* (Sussex: Harvester Press).

Jahoda, M. (1977) *Freud and the Dilemmas of Psychology* (London: The Hogarth Press).

Jones, K. (unpublished) *Professional Skills and Patients' Needs* (Lecture given to Royal College of Psychiatrists, 25 February 1983).

Kovel, J. (1981) 'The American Mental Health Industry', in Ingleby D., (ed.) *Critical Psychiatry* (Harmondsworth: Penguin).

Lacan, J. (1977) *Ecrits: A Selection* (London: Tavistock).

Laing, R. D. (1959) *The Divided Self* (Harmondsworth: Penguin).

Laing, R. D. (1961) *Self and Others* (Harmondsworth: Penguin).

Laing, R. D. (1967) *The Politics of Experience* (Harmondsworth: Penguin).

Laing, R. D. & Esterson, A. (1964) *Sanity, Madness and the Family* (Harmondsworth: Penguin).

Lasch, C. (1982) *The Culture of Narcissism* (London: Abacus).

Leonard, P. (1984) *Personality and Ideology- Toward a Materialist Understanding of the Institutional* (London: Macmillan).

Lewellyn, S. & Kelly, J. (1980) 'Individualism in Psychology: A Case for a new Paradigm?', *Bulletin of the British Psychological Society* No. 33, pp. 407–11.

Llewellyn, S. & Osborne, K. :1983) 'Women as Clients and Therapists', in *Psychology and Psychotherapy, Current Issues*, Pilgrim D., (ed.) (London: Routledge & Kegan Paul).

London-Edinburgh Weekend Return Group (1979) *In and Against the State* (pamphlet).

Lukárs, G. (1971) *History and Class Consciousness: Studies in Marxist Dialectics* (London: Merlin).

Marcuse, H. (1955) *Eros and Civilisation* (Boston: Beacon Press).

Menzies, I. (1960) *The Functioning of Social Systems as a Defence against Anxiety* (Tavistock Pamphlet No. 3).

Mind (1983) *Common Concern: MIND's Manifesto for a new Mental Health Service* (London: MIND Publications).

Mitchell, J. (1974) *Psychoanalysis and Feminism* (Harmondsworth: Penguin).

Park, R. (1952) *Human Communities: The City and Human Ecology* (New York: The Free Press).

Ramon, S. (1983) 'Psychiatria Democratica: A Case Study of an Italian Community Mental Health Service', *International Journal of Health Services*, No. 13, pp. 307–24.

Reich, W. (1975) *The Mass Psychology of Fascism* (Harmondsworth: Penguin).

Riley, D. (1978) 'Developmental Psychology: Biology and Marxism', *Ideology and Consciousness*, 4, pp. 73–92.

Rutter, M. & Madge, N. (1976) *Cycles of Disadvantage* (London: Heinemann).

Rutter, M., Yule, B., Quinton, D., Rowlands, O., Yule, W. & Berger, M. (1975) 'Attainment and Adjustment in Two Geographical Areas: III Some Factors

Accounting for Area Differences', *British Journal of Psychiatry*, 126, pp. 520–33.

Sedgwick, P. (1982) *Psychopolitics* (London: Pluto Press).

Segal, H. (1964) *Introduction to the Work of Melanie Klein* (London: The Hogarth Press).

Segal, L. (1983) 'Sensual Uncertainty, or Why the Clitoris is not Enough', in Cartledge, S. & Ryan, J. (eds) *Sex and Love* (London: The Women's Press).

Séve, L. (1978) *Man in Marxist Theroy* (Sussex: Harvester).

Shepherd, G. (1984) *Institutional Care and Rehabilitation* (Harlow: Longman).

Skinner, B. F. (1971) *Beyond Freedom and Dignity* (Harmondsworth: Penguin).

Watts, F. & Bennett, D. (eds) (1984) *The Theory and Practice of Psychiatric Rehabilitation* (Chichester: Wiley).

Wollheim, R. (1971) *Freud* (London: Fontana Modern Masters).

World Health Organisation (1979) *Schizophrenia: An International Follow-Up Study* (Chichester: Wiley).

Index